How
Theatre
Happens

How Theatre Happens

Stephen M. Archer

UNIVERSITY OF MISSOURI,
COLUMBIA

Macmillan Publishing Co., Inc.
NEW YORK

Macmillan Publishing Co., Inc.
866 Third Avenue, New York, New York 10022

Collier Macmillan Canada, Ltd.

Library of Congress Cataloging in Publication Data

Archer, Stephen M
  How theatre happens.

  Bibliography: p.
  Includes index.
  1. Theater.   I. Title.
PN2037.A597   792'.015   77-22866
ISBN 0-02-303830-6

Printing: 1 2 3 4 5 6 7 8   Year: 8 9 0 1 2 3 4

Preface

*"The multitude of books is a great evil. There is
no measure or limit to this fever of writing;
everyone must be an author; some out of vanity to
acquire celebrity; others for the sake of lucre and
gain."*

—Martin Luther, *Table-Talk*

This book is intended for students in theatre appreciation courses. Such courses vary widely as to specifics of en-
rollment, configuration, and intention but in many cases
center around an examination of how the theatre happens.
This book examines the contemporary theatre. I hope it will
stimulate further discussion and examination appropriate
to the reader's specific circumstances.

Chapter One seeks to put the art of the theatre into a
perspective with human activity in general and the other
fine arts specifically. Of necessity the most abstract of the
chapters, it suggests why the theatre continues to attract audiences in the face of electronic media and other stimuli we
encounter daily. The text next examines the major contributors to the theatrical event: the playwright, the director,
the actor, the designers, and the architect. Each of these
chapters is divided into five sections. The first, on artistic alternatives and restrictions, seeks to describe the boundaries
for the individual artist, or where his work begins and

where others take over. The second section, on requisites for excellence, describes the personal qualities and training needed to succeed in that particular theatrical position. The third section, which covers the contemporary situation, describes the circumstances under which the modern theatre artist works. Creative procedures are described in the fourth section: how each theatre artist goes about his work and what steps he takes to create his contribution to production. The last section of these chapters, on evaluating the artist's contribution, involves separating each theatre artist's work from the others and discovering some basis for judging the quality of his work. The five sections are used in Chapters Two through Six; Chapters One and Seven have different organization.

I cannot restrain the professor in me from offering a few bits of advice as you begin. First, be alert to the diversity found in the theatre; the rich variety of theatrical styles represents much of its appeal. You will surely be asked to attend theatrical performances if you are enrolled in a theatre-appreciation course; you may go one evening to a traditional performance in a traditional theatre and the next evening to a performance in a converted basement in which the production violates most traditions. No matter, both are theatre.

Second, seek to discover the intricate interaction of the various theatrical elements. Just as in music some instruments supply basics and some supply embellishments, in the theatre the elements of script, acting, and design interact in shifting configurations to offer a new work of art at every performance. Examining these relationships will do much to enrich your own theatregoing.

Above all, test what you read here against your actual experiences in the theatre, just as you would test any proffered theory against the reality you encounter. If the gap between what you find in this book and what you observe seems wider than you think it should be, try to find out why. Seek other opinions; no one person can experience, let alone describe, the total spectrum of the theatre. And no book can hope to substitute for an articulate and informed teacher; a book can only, and that is the hope here, offer another viewpoint to throw the problem areas into sharper focus.

While I have read many acknowledgments in prefaces such as this, not until completion of this manuscript did I realize how many persons contribute to a book's publication. I have deeply appreciated the continuing and substantial support of Professor Sam Smiley for several years now; his encouragement has meant a great deal to me. Lloyd Chilton and J. Edward Neve of Macmillan have been continually patient and understanding throughout the whole endeavor. Many of my friends and colleagues have generously assisted in several ways: Larry Clark, John Cooper, Peter Sargent, Richard Lorenzen, Michael Hardy of the Krannert Center, Charlotte Guindon of the Guthrie Theatre, the theatre faculty of Southern Illinois University–Edwardsville, Marianne Janauer of the Max Reinhardt Archives, Henry Tharp, Margaret Kielley of United Scenic Artists, Charron Traut of Western Springs, Connie Dawson and Sama Swaminathan of the Royal Shakespeare Company: to all I offer my deep thanks.

Finally, offering gratitude to one's family has become a cliché, but Kelly and Steven have proved the truth of it, beyond the call of duty.

S. M. A.

Contents

CONTENTS

x

Chapter One

☆

Art and
the Theatre

"You can safely ignore the arts and sciences. They never helped anybody."
—Kurt Vonnegut, *God Gless You, Mr. Rosewater*

Once upon a time, a great Italian actress, Eleanora Duse (1859–1924), became a major star on the European continent. Duse later came to the United States for a tour. Upon her return to Europe, she pointed out with horror, "In America they *teach* art!" adding, "Anyone who presumes to *teach* art has no understanding of it."

Duse might well have mistrusted education. As the daughter of traveling actors, she received almost no formal schooling; when she did attend classes, the other students ridiculed her as an outcast. Her immense native intelligence found no fulfillment in the schools available to her, although she later taught herself to read and educated herself in that way.

Perhaps under those circumstances, one might well be suspicious of studying art; when one considers the artistic experience as a revealing, intimate interaction between two or more human beings, one might as well study lovemaking. Considering further, the blatant capitalism of the United

1

States may seem to some to contrast sharply with the aesthetic and subjective values of art.

Yet we find ourselves in an age of expansion for the arts in the United States. Indeed, a recent poll concludes that serious participation in the arts now exceeds our participation in sports. In New York State alone, attendance in 1976 at nonprofit professional arts events exceeded 75 million, whereas attendance at professional sports events was only 22 million.

A few more statistics will even further substantiate claims of the increase in artistic endeavor in this country. A recent report by the National Committee for Cultural Resources suggests that interest in the arts has risen steadily over the past decade and shows every indication of continuing. The committee cites as evidence such figures as the following: (1) the number of professional dance companies with budgets over $100,000 has risen from fewer than ten to fifty; (2) the number of resident, nonprofit professional theatres has grown from thirty to fifty; (3) museums are drawing a record attendance, aided by special displays, traveling exhibits, and other imaginative new programs; (4) half of the major symphony orchestras now provide year-round, rather than seasonal, employment for their members; and (5) the number of students enrolled in arts courses in universities and colleges is rising.

The committee further points out that state appropriations in support of the arts have increased from $1.7 million to $55 million in the last ten years, and the appropriation for the National Endowment for the Arts has risen from $2.5 million in 1966 to over $74.7 million in 1975. The committee suggests many reasons for these increases, among them (1) the increase in leisure time; (2) widening exposure to the arts through television and radio; (3) greater emphasis on the arts in education; and (4) a deepening awareness of the contribution the arts make to the quality and spirit of American life.

The National Research Center of the Arts made the first

FIGURE 1-1. *The exterior of the Tyrone Guthrie Theatre, Minneapolis, Minnesota. This theatre, founded by and named after the famous English director, achieved new levels of excellence in regional theatre in this country. Permission from the Tyrone Guthrie Theatre.*

in-depth survey of the public's attitude toward the arts in January 1973, then repeated the survey in June 1975, employing in-depth personal interviews of a representative sample of the United States population. The public's evaluation of the arts, strongly positive in 1973, rose even higher, as evidenced by the following: (1) those who believe that museums, theatres, concert halls, and like facilities are important to the quality of life in a community rose from 89 to 93 percent, and (2) those who believe that arts and cultural facilities are important to the business and economy of the community rose from 80 to 85 percent. In questions throughout the survey, the public indicated time and again

3

its belief that the arts are central to life in America today. In 1972 experts estimated more than 60 million Americans visited our art museums, 12 million attended symphony concerts, and more than $2 billion was spent annually on cultural activities. The next year an estimated 46 million people attended the theatre at least once, more than 30 million went to the opera, and 20 million went to symphony concerts. Museum attendance approached 70 million, and ballet and modern dance 12 million.

Space does not permit a survey of world history with regard to art, but even a quick glance at man's heritage from the beginning of recorded history indicates that no society, however primitive or spartan, has existed without its unique art forms and endeavors, reflecting with considerable accuracy the particular circumstances of that social unit. Even the repressive Greek city of Sparta, which held all pleasure in contempt, retained choral dance and music, forms that could display Spartan discipline, losing all individualism in the mass. Architecture of some form was, of course, mandatory. And none mourned when the Spartans fell from power; their contempt of pleasure led an ancient writer to suggest, "It was not a commendable thing in them to be so ready to die in the wars, since by that they were freed from much hard labor and miserable living." Nazi Germany similarly distorted the functions of art but retained the external forms and plundered conquered nations as others had before.

The Function of Art

Why has art, which seems to some effete, extraneous, and impractical, commanded so much of world's concern, and why have many of the finest minds and talents produced by humanity been attracted to it? To find art's purposes and justifications, one may learn much from an examination of

4

FIGURE 1-2. *Johann Wolfgang von Goethe (1749–1832).*

art's functions and their effect upon recipients. Among the clearer and more useful discussions of such matters is the work of Johann Wolfgang von Goethe (1749–1832), a German poet, playwright, theoretician, novelist, and scientist. Goethe proposed that art had three possible functions: (1)

entertainment, (2) edification, and (3) exaltation of the human spirit. These three functions, amplified in the following sections, comprise absolute essentials for human existence, essentials that may be obtained from nonartistic sources, to be sure, but essentials found in rich supply in the arts in general and in theatre in particular. Art thus emerges as more than merely "cultural enrichment"; it has served the basic needs of humanity and has exerted a constant influence upon centuries of human existence.

ENTERTAINMENT

Entertainment may not seem a basic human requirement until one considers a life without it. Just as dreams supply a psychic safety valve, so we all require diversion for relief from seemingly more important matters, such as money, grades, survival, reproduction, and the like. Entertainment, usually thought of as mere amusement or titillation, involves more complex matters. The word itself comes from the Latin *tenere,* "to hold," and a complete definition suggests "to hold the attention agreeably." The variety and relativity of what different people find agreeable implies a wide spectrum of entertainment possibilities, not at all restricted to the arts. Major-league sports, for example, not usually considered as aesthetic endeavors, undeniably require considerable skill for their execution and experience for their full appreciation. Sporting events supply rich entertainment to literally millions of spectators.

If nonartistic forms and events often supply entertainment, the fine arts must comparably appeal to their audiences. Even so blatantly political and didactic a playwright as Bertolt Brecht stated flatly in *A Little Organum for the Theatre,* "From the first it has been the theatre's business to entertain people, as it also has of all the other arts. . . . Nothing needs less justification than pleasures." While this concept may seem obvious, some persons have felt that the

6

ideal life requires stoicism and asceticism. Such concepts, now usually considered sterile, deny the pleasurable aspects of art and life.

Many people find beauty chief among the pleasures derived from art. Beauty as a concept in art stimulates considerable debate and discussion; indeed, some critics of the "art for art's sake" school deplore functional approaches to aesthetics and art, proposing the pursuit of the beautiful as the only proper concern of the artist. Because beauty can be described as a harmonious unity that gives the recipient pleasure and thereby holds his attention agreeably, beauty as an aesthetic concept relates most directly to Goethe's suggestion of entertainment as an artistic function. Beauty, of course, frequently occurs outside art works; a mountain range such as the Grand Tetons or a stunning sunset may overwhelm the viewer with its visual beauty. Moreover, not all artists seek to create beauty in their work; some pursue other functions of art as their primary goals. Nevertheless, beauty as a quality of art remains of major concern.

EDIFICATION

Edification as a function of art may at first seem less obvious. Most people do not seek out artistic experiences to learn something; critics have called the theatre a house of emotion rather than intellect. Yet human survival itself requires constant acquisition of knowledge. Most obviously, the newborn infant intellectually knows practically nothing but begins learning survival and social techniques at birth and continues to do so throughout his existence. Our educational systems may sometimes corrode the sheer love of learning and the absorption of new experiences in the young person, but most people, young or old, find new insights into themselves and the world around them immensely gratifying and hence entertaining. Thus the categories of entertainment, edification, and exaltation begin

7

to merge and emerge as only slightly different facets of human response. A particular form of edification may prove quite entertaining to a specific individual and a total bore to another. For example, a stamp collector may derive great pleasure from his hobby and may find delight in information about printing, economy, political and social history, engraving, and so on, as it relates to assembling such a collection. Such activity may well bore another person senseless and drive him to considerable lengths to avoid it. Similarly, rare-book collectors, sports-car buffs, hunters, "Star Trek" fans, and even sports fans will not find universal enthusiasm for their various interests.

The varieties of edification further cloud its consideration as an artistic function. Cerebral, intellectual, or factual learning constitutes only one sort of edification; the viewer of an artwork may well come away from the experience with a wider point of view or a change in his attitudes about some aspect of human endeavor. The widely admired television movie, *Roots,* based on Alex Haley's brilliant book, may well teach the viewer something about slavery, the old South, or African villages, but much more importantly, the film delineates man's inhumanity to man and the human being's ability to absorb and conquer adversity. Such a film or book is not so much *about* something as it *is* something, an artwork capable of adding a dimension to a viewer's perception of existence, giving him an emotional awareness he may never obtain in any other way. This awareness does not correspond to a "moral" or a "theme"; if art were that simple, a bare statement would be enough. The experience of the artwork, not a stark paraphrase, can lead to increased sensitivity and sympathy with one's fellow human beings.

EXALTATION

Goethe's third function of art, exaltation, strikes many people as a far more difficult concept than the first two. Exaltation is usually associated with religion rather than art, but scholars often point out the common origins of religion and art, an attempt to define, order, understand, and thus control a dimly perceived, often misunderstood environment. Primitive man did not distinguish between art, religion, and science as he sought understanding of his surroundings.

Religion properly concerns itself with man's relationship with his gods. Art, on the other hand, deals with man's relationships with himself, his fellowmen, and his existence. Much of the world's greatest art depicts the magnificence of the human spirit, especially when faced with adversity. Consider, for example, Michelangelo's statue of "David," depicting the biblical hero as he turns to face Goliath. For many, the entertainment value of this artwork lies in its imitation of life, the recognition of the human form Michelangelo brilliantly wrested from the marble in heroic scale. When one learns that the artist sculpted this masterpiece from a marble slab rejected by several other artists, the work becomes even more technically impressive. Further investigation can reveal the metaphorical nature of the statue; more than just a biblical event is depicted when one considers the nature of Renaissance man, specifically the citizens of Florence, who, like David, had to fight off hostile forces to survive as leaders of northern Italy during the Renaissance. And in the largest sense, "David" presents a position statement about man's eternal battle with opposing forces; such a depiction glorifies a humanity that must do battle over and over again to achieve any worthwhile goal. The exaltation that can result from viewing "David" has brought millions of people to a wider and higher view of humanity and themselves.

Another example of art's capacity for spiritual exaltation emerges from Sophocles's *Oedipus Rex,* written about 427 B.C. In this famous tragedy, Oedipus discovers he has committed a hideous although unintentional series of crimes. Social and political destruction follow; from being King of Thebes, fate reduces him to an exiled beggar; Oedipus

9

blinds himself in punishment for his sins when he accepts his guilt. Paradoxically, he achieves a spiritual victory in the face of what seems a total defeat; this victory in defeat reveals to the audience his greatness of spirit. A life without spiritual awareness has not achieved its human potential; art can stimulate that awareness. The search for that awareness has led humanity to varying sources, from Zen to LSD, indicating a universal need for the transcendental state. In

FIGURE 1-3. *Michelangelo's masterpiece, "David," depicts the Biblical hero as he turns to confront Goliath. Photograph by the author.*

tragedy, perhaps the highest form of dramatic literature, all the pettiness, the bestiality, and the littleness of humanity is blasted out of the protagonist, revealing him in his most human and humane state, far beyond the trifles of everyday life. He suffers monumentally, but he suffers as only a human being can suffer, revealing to the viewer the scope of the human spirit in a state most of us will never encounter. This conceptual revelation gives satisfaction to the audience, and a well-performed and well-received *Oedipus Rex* offers living proof of the interaction between entertainment, edification, and exaltation of the human spirit.

If the nature of human existence requires entertainment and edification, so too does it require some form of exaltation. Just as the individual must have confidence and self-respect in order to face his existence, so too must he have a wide view of humanity as it struggles toward its destiny, beset by the trivial and the mundane.

Art can supply humanity with three necessities: stimulating diversion, insight into the human condition, and humanistic spiritual exaltation. Obviously other sources offer these qualities: nature, religion, philosophy, and education offer comparable rewards. Any human activity profoundly approached can profoundly reward; an individual could conceivably discover as much about the nature of man from a stock-car race as from an art gallery. The artist more obviously seeks aesthetic ends, however, and that art has supplied insight, entertainment, and spiritual growth to millions of persons simply cannot be denied.

People seek out the fine arts in the hope that their lives will be better for the experience. Viewed from the widest vantage point, art supplies a more ordered view of existence than can be derived from day-to-day existence; the artist differs from the nonartist in his ability to depict and interpret life in aesthetic form.

In the final analysis, art is a response to one's environment, offered to the public with the hope of bringing a wider view of existence into being. Hemingway called writ-

11

ing a hunt for a truth worth expressing; the resultant expression can offer considerable insight and awareness to its audience. Although much human endeavor, artistic or not, fails, art can supply the essential entertainment, edification, and exaltation to millions and thereby substantially increase the quality of life. A society without art is unthinkable and has indeed never existed. No one can therefore safely ignore such a pivotal facet of human life; every thinking and feeling person sooner or later must come to grips with the artistic transaction and what it can offer him, while realizing that the wide diversity of artistic options will challenge him in the most significant ways.

Toward a Definition of Theatre

The widely varying forms of theatre seem to prohibit exact definition; even among theatre workers, discussion often results in expression of diverse points of view about the theatre's exact nature and function. Definitions of theatre are usually either too simple to be helpful or too restrictive to be accurate; theatre involves an ever-widening spectrum of dramatic activity. Traditionally, theatre has been thought to occur when actors appear on a stage and perform a story for an audience, but even so simple a statement leads to fairly complex distinctions. If, for example, the actors and the audience are separated in space, as in radio drama or live television, is this theatre? If the stage and the audience are separated in both time and space, as in video-taped drama or film, can one legitimately consider either dramatic form as theatre?

This text will consider only the more traditional theatre, in which actors and audience coexist in the same place at the same time. This approach implies distinction from rather than denigration of either television or film; both viable and dynamic art forms can offer enormous aesthetic

12

impact. But the essential quality of the traditional theatre stems from its immediacy: only in the live theatre can actor and audience achieve the sort of communion sought in every performance; only in the living theatre can immediate feedback and circular response between performer and audience occur. The film or video actor, however talented, can do nothing to alter his performance after it has been edited and recorded; indeed, many film and video actors never experience an audience's reaction to their work, although several television shows tape before live audiences. The stage actor, on the other hand, receives immediate response from his audience and usually alters or modifies his performance for a particular audience. Further, he has greater potential for control over his audience because of this immediacy; he can have the impact of a living human being as opposed to that of a projected image. This potential will be explored further in Chapter Four.

Theatre's Relationship to the Other Fine Arts

Further confusion about the nature of theatre emerges from its apparent dependence upon the other fine arts; to the casual onlooker, theatre often seems a conglomerate of several other arts rather than a distinct art in and of itself. For example, literary scholars frequently study scripts as literature, quite apart from their theatrical function. But playwrights almost never write their scripts for solitary reading; they write instead for live performance on a stage by actors for an audience. Any successful playwright will attest to the sharp distinction in style, form, and content for an author who aims at live performance rather than at the individual reader. The relationship compares with that of a film scenario to a completed film; the former constitutes part of the latter; it offers a plan or outline or intention for achieving the latter but is in no way a complete artwork in itself. Literary critical techniques usually help illuminate the playwright's work, to be sure, but the playwright seeks a goal sharply distinct from that of the novelist or the poet.

Comparably, scenic artists do a great deal of painting in the theatre; backdrops, murals, act curtains, or two-dimensional scenery often call for detailed and meticulous painting. But theatrical painting, although it may call for many of the same techniques used by the easel painter, has a distinctly different purpose and should not be judged in the same way as easel painting. The contribution to the eventual production forms the evaluative basis for theatrical painting; how it strikes one as an artwork by itself is coincidental and largely irrelevant.

So, too, the principles of sculpture often find function in the theatre in the arrangement of the actors in the performance space, in some forms of scenic design, and in some makeup constructions. Again, one should not confuse the techniques of an art with the art itself; sculpture and theatre, although they may sometimes share techniques, remain separate arts.

Music and dance, being performing arts themselves, can create even more confusion in this regard. Quite often, music is composed and dance is choreographed specifically for theatrical performance; the unwary frequently evaluate them quite apart from the total performance. Again, only the contribution of the music or the dance to the theatrical production should determine its success or failure. A magnificent musical work might well seem totally inappropriate to a given production. Beethoven's Fifth Symphony, rightfully considered a masterpiece, might seem an unwise choice as an overture for a Neil Simon comedy. "Cabaret" was a climactic musical number in both the stage play and the film, but one might not care to use it as background music for *Macbeth* or *Oklahoma!* To add to the confusion, a song from a show, such as "Cabaret," may succeed handsomely on its own as a hit record. In this case, the song, part

14

of a larger artwork, the production, is separated from it to win or lose favor on its own.

Finally, architecture and theatre may seem at first glance to have little in common, but scenic designers find themselves studying construction procedures in order to place accurate representations on stage; sometimes they employ standard construction techniques. More importantly, the architect's design in theatre construction has practical and functional effects upon all facets of theatre production, as described in Chapter Six.

Overall, then, one must consider the wide spectrum of activities within a theatre only in the theatrical context, not as an accumulation of borrowed techniques from other arts. The final evaluation comes when an audience views the results of the theatrical preparation. Any critical statement prior to that time constitutes prophesy and, although often helpful to the theatre artist, should be considered as such. Theatre, then, emerges not as a conglomeration of arts but as a distinct art form that exists only in the actual production of a play for an audience.

The distinction of the theatre from other performing arts seems to center on the inherent and self-imposed limitations of those other arts. Dance and mime employ movement to the exclusion of other human action, although music usually supports the movement. Music itself as a performing art restricts itself to nonverbal sound in most cases; vocal music frequently approximates an actor relating a story to an audience from a stage. Opera and musical comedy are theatrical by any definition of the term, although opera involves such complexity that it is often studied separately, and the musical aspects frequently dominate the total effect. Nevertheless, operatic composers clearly conceive their works to be performed on a stage for audiences in a shared social environment.

The art of the theatre emerges as separate and distinct from the other six fine arts; as a performing art, its living nature remains its essential quality. While sharing many

15

techniques with other arts, theatre is capable of delineating the human condition in the most overtly humanistic manifestations of any of the arts.

The Complexities of Theatre Art

As a performing art, theatre has the advantages of life and the disadvantages of death; it exists only in performance and dies as the performance ends. A further complication emerges from the theatre's need for repetition; one showing of a play rarely justifies the necessary effort or expense, so the production company usually must repeat it for successive audiences. The problems inherent in this repetition do not trouble the film or video actor; once his performance is filmed or taped, he has finished his work, but the stage actor faces the audience's challenge again and again, as often as eight times a week in the modern commercial theatre.

But, in fact, an event cannot be repeated exactly; thus the theatre artist, especially the actor, confronts a further set of problems. Audiences differ, and each audience modifies the production. Human personalities change from day to day, and actors have, like athletes, good days and bad ones. Theatre artists speak of good and bad audiences; some audiences simply have greater collective perception and responsiveness than others; some give the actors nothing to which they can respond; others are capable of rich reaction to the theatrical event and thereby stimulate the performers' best work. Each performing artist faces the same probelm, and anyone who has rehearsed in an empty auditorium knows what a difference the audience makes to his work.

Further, the commercial aspects of the audience have major effects upon production. Because theatre literally cannot exist without an audience, it depends upon its ap-

16

peal to the potential audience of the production's time and place. In the commercial theatre, audience acceptance determines the life or death of the production; commercial producers commonly invest enormous amounts of money, leading them to minimize fiscal risks. For example, backers invested $650,000 several years ago in a musical comedy, *Kelly*. The show opened out of New York, arrived on Broadway after a good deal of trouble, and closed after one performance.

Being a communal art, the theatre requires the work of a wide variety of people with the resultant need for successful human interaction, communication, compromise, and sharing of vision. To begin with, the traditional theatrical forms require playwrights, directors, designers, architects, actors, and, of course, the audience. This book will approach each of these contributors in successive chapters, but this is by no means a definitive list. Also involved in production and performance are producers, critics, stage managers, prompters, assistants to the director, makeup artists, property crews, publicists, publicity designers, box-office personnel, ushers, special-effects designers, security personnel, and so on, all contributing to a greater or lesser degree to a production's success. Audiences rarely see most of these people, but their work undeniably affects audience reception of a production.

The Theatrical Spectrum

The wide spectrum of theatrical and theatrelike activities can sometimes confuse the theatrical newcomer. If the working definition of the theatre as a story related by actors from a stage to an audience indeed has any value, certain other human actions also seem basically theatrical. Consider, for example, the ritual of the Roman Catholic High Mass, in which costumed performers (the priest and the altar boys) appear on a platform before a congregation–audience and enact a highly conventionalized narrative of the death and resurrection of Christ. Clearly, the Mass seeks religious and not primarily aesthetic ends, but if spiritual exaltation is a proper function of art and theatre, many common elements link the theatre and religious ritual. And, indeed, congregations find some Masses more moving, more effective, more exalting, and thus more theatrical than others; all the elements of theatre come into play.

In sporting events, one can also find commonalities with theatre. In major-league football, costumed performers resolve a conflict in a playing area before an assembled audience. Although the performers have practiced for the event, no actual football game exists until the conflict begins, and unless a fix is on, no one knows the result in advance. Theatrical performances are usually scripted and the outcome of the narrative predetermined, but, comparably, the event is not actual until presented to an audience. No one seriously proposes football and other major-league sports as theatre, but their relationship to and role in the entertainment industry and "show business" indicates some comparable appeals to their audiences.

Even street violence and public demonstrations have theatrical aspects. Again, the event is real, not staged, in most cases, and no one can do more than attempt prediction of the conflict's resolution. Again, participants enter a space to resolve a conflict, usually surrounded by onlookers. The line between performer and onlooker sometimes blurs, and people pass from one category to another as an observer is swept into the melee. The goal is not aesthetic, so street demonstrations cannot be considered as art, entertainment, or show business, but some structural and ritualistic commonalities unmistakably present themselves.

To sum up the spectrum of theatrical activities, one may say that theatre exists in any consciously aesthetic attempt to delineate human existence for an audience in a performance presented by living actors to a living audience. Tra-

18

ditional theatre is verbal, narrative, and usually conflict-centered, but it doesn't depend exclusively on any of those qualities.

Producing Agencies

The variety of producing agencies, situations, and motivations also presents a wide spectrum; people create theatre for many reasons and in many different circumstances.

Most people equate the professional theatre with the Broadway theatre in New York City. Although a decentralization process seems under way, New York still contains the most significant portion of the American theatre, at least in the minds of most audience members. Severe production situations prevail; a New York producer must deal with approximately two dozen labor unions in order to stage a production. This situation has led to escalation of both production costs and ticket prices.

At the time this book is being written, for example, the most expensive ticket on Broadway purchased at the box office costs $17.50 (Saturday evening orchestra seats for *Annie, I Love My Wife,* or *A Chorus Line,* all popular musicals). *Grease* has a top ticket at $15.90. Nonmusicals, although not commanding so high a price, have a top price of $15 (*California Suite, Equus*). Even the Off-Broadway offerings, which used to be considerably cheaper, offered *Godspell* at $9.90, *The Hot l Baltimore* at $8.50, and *A Midsummer Night's Dream* at $8.00. Perhaps more significantly, the lowest price one might pay to enter a Broadway theatre is $6, although one might occasionally find a cheaper seat Off-Broadway. These figures change frequently; the reader can find current prices in the *New York Times* or similar publications.

Broadway backers face an unusual circumstance for financial speculation, that of being totally wiped out and los-

19

ing their entire investment. Because total investments may approach $1 million, fiscal prudence must subordinate aesthetic choices; too much capital is at stake.

If producers on Broadway run substantial risks, they can also win enormous rewards. *Cabaret* cost a half million to stage and cleared a profit of $1.74 million. A $400,000 investment in *My Fair Lady* returned nearly $12 million. Even though four out of five Broadway shows fail, and even though costs continue to escalate, investors come forward with the money. One of Broadway's most successful producers, Hal Prince, as of 1972 had produced nineteen shows, out of which eight were flops. But whereas he lost $1.5 million on the flops, his successful shows (*Fiddler on the Roof, Follies, Cabaret, Damn Yankees, West Side Story,* and so on) profited ten times that much. With a success ratio of just over 50 percent, his investors have received a 230 percent profit. Truly, there is no business quite like show business. Although musicals cost more to produce and offer greater potential reward, a comparable set of circumstances exists for nonmusical Broadway offerings.

Educational theatre usually refers to productions generated by universities, colleges, and secondary and primary schools. In most cases, the difference between the educational and the aesthetic functions of production must be resolved by the participants in order to clarify goals. Educational theatre usually entails much lower budgets, salaries, and ticket prices because nonunion or even nonsalaried personnel do the bulk of the work.

Most university and college theatre departments seek to increase their students' understanding of the theatre, and most find a combination of classroom study and production the most efficient means. Some universities tend to emphasize one aspect, some the other; the best seek a balance between "academic" and "practical" study of theatre.

The apparent distinction between academic and practical does not bear up under examination, however. Practice without theory seems impossible because action reveals theory or philosophy in practice. Colleges and universities properly offer first a wide and liberal education and second vocational preparation, at least on the undergraduate level. At the graduate level, the M.A., Ph.D., and Ed.D. programs prepare the student for teaching and scholarly careers; the M.F.A. and the rarer D.F.A. and D.A., such as offered by the Goodman School of Drama in Chicago or the Juilliard School in New York, are usually terminal degrees in production techniques and exemplify the conservatory approach. Such institutions primarily restrict work to acting, directing, design, playwriting, and so on and consider their productions as laboratory work. Perhaps the most successful of such operations is the Royal Academy of Dramatic Art in London; many of the major British theatre artists studied at RADA.

Secondary schools or high schools also offer fundamental theatre training to their students. These programs vary widely, from well-budgeted departments of a dozen faculty with lavish facilities to situations in which a teacher, with minimal if any theatre experience, agrees to direct a class play in a gymnasium or cafeteria. Again, the student is more-or-less prepared for further study. The quality of the program depends, naturally, upon the training and talents of the supervisory personnel and the support given to them by the school administration. Most state governments do not offer certification for high-school teachers of theatre and include the discipline instead with speech or English.

Children's theatre, another form of dramatic art, grows rapidly in importance in the United States today. Currently an increasing number of theatre artists are finding rewards and satisfaction in children's theatre; administrators begin to see the worth of such work, and the future bodes well for this facet of theatre.

Community theatre usually allies with neither the professional nor the educational theatre; it is rather an avocational theatre in that most of the participants do not take part for money but more often out of their affection for the art.

21

Production expenses sometimes force community theatre groups to scrimp and employ severely reductive shortcuts. Most community groups must rent or borrow a theatre in which to perform, but some groups, such as the Theatre of Western Springs in the Chicago suburbs, have been so successful as to build enviable theatre plants and continue to stage well-received productions. In the early part of this century, little-theatre groups succeeded in bringing remarkable innovations to the American theatre, and they continue to serve as a vital and dynamic part of the total theatre scene.

Nonaesthetic orientations can also exist in the theatre—that is, the production of plays for other than artistic purposes. Because function determines form and because no one should be criticized for not doing what he had no intention of doing, discussion of such groups requires different evaluation criteria.

Creative dramatics, perhaps the best known of such endeavors, involves the use of acting situations—sometimes leading to production, sometimes not—in order to lead the child to a wider view of himself during his formative years. The act of spontaneous creation, as in improvisatory acting, opens the youthful psyche when properly executed. Creative dramatics seeks developmental rather than artistic goals and thus requires no audience for successful completion.

Psychodrama traditionally concerns adults rather than children, usually adults with psychological difficulties. Acting out aggression or repression may assist the actor–patient to self-realization and thus to a more satisfactory life. Once more, personal development rather than aesthetic satisfaction results; psychodrama as a technique rather than an art is coming more and more into use as psychological treatment.

Finally, religious drama occupies a unique place in the theatrical spectrum. These productions range from short plays presented during church services to the enormous

FIGURE 1-4A. *An exterior view of the Theatre of Western Springs. This community theatre, located in a Chicago suburb, represents the high level of achievement often reached by avocational theatre. Permission from the Theatre of Western Springs.*

FIGURE 1-4B. *The interior of the Theatre of Western Springs. The steeply raked seating area allows the spectators a clear view of the thrust stage, upon which the actors are rehearsing. As can be seen behind the actors, the theatre also possesses proscenium capability. Permission from the Theatre of Western Springs.*

Passion Plays in several American communities (Normal, Illinois; Spearfish, South Dakota; Lake Wales, Florida) and often seek theologically didactic rather than aesthetic audience impact, although the resultant productions often move their audiences deeply. Dramatization of biblical narratives began as early as 1000 A.D. and dominated western European drama for five or six centuries; the Church literally kept the theatre alive after the Fall of Rome. Today, religious drama constitutes a relatively minor form, but more and more churches utilize the appeal of theological edification through enactment, and some trained personnel find their theatrical destinies in this type of drama.

Conclusions

In overview, then, the theatre emerges as a distinct art with multiple functions as varied as man's nature itself. Above all, however, the theatre emerges as a viable and dynamic potential source of meeting man's needs as expressed by Goethe: entertainment, edification, and exaltation. The widespread need for diversion has led to the development of farce and musical comedy, frequently productions with entertainment as their primary goal. Serious drama and comedy offer entertainment plus emotional and cerebral insights into the human condition. Tragedy most overtly seeks the realm of exaltation of the human spirit experiencing and conquering adversity in the face of physical and social destruction. Although other arts and other human institutions supply comparable satisfactions to humanity, the theatre, with its unique living dynamism, continues to offer its uniqe qualities and values to humanity.

Perhaps Tennessee Williams put it best when asked during a television interview to express what was the purpose of his work or what he wanted people to realize after experiencing his scripts. Williams thought a bit, then drawled, "That other people have been through it, too."

Chapter Two

The Playwright

"For a student has essentially the same task as the poet; to make clear to himself, and thereby to others, the temporal and eternal questions which are astir in the age and in the community to which he belongs."
—HENRIK IBSEN, *"Speech to the Norwegian Students, September 10, 1874."*

IN a draw-poker game, the odds against being dealt a full house in the first five cards are about 588 to 1. A full house (three of a kind and a pair, such as three aces and two eights) will usually win the pot, but not always.

Playwrights face similar odds. Americans write approximately ten thousand full-length scripts a year, only a few hundred of which are seriously considered for production. Of those scripts produced, only one in ten will achieve any kind of success. As Moss Hart once said, "Playwriting, like begging in India, is an honorable but humbling profession."

But if the odds against success are formidable, so are the potential rewards. Neil Simon has probably earned more money than any playwright in the history of the world by appealing to hundreds of thousands of theatregoers and millions of film and TV viewers. A few others make comfortable livings with their scripts, but the United States has far more professional poker players than professional playwrights; the odds are better.

Yet the playwright's efforts literally generate the theatre. We may have difficulty imagining playwrights such as Sophocles or Shakespeare actually sitting down to blank papyrus or paper, but every playwright begins with nothing, whereas other theatre artists usually work in response to the playwright's creation. The playwright has for this reason traditionally been considered the primary theatrical artist.

Playwrights not only supply the language for the production but first concoct the dramatic situations that take place on stage. The word *plot* has a double meaning, describing both what happens on stage and also the playwright's scheme or plan for the play; the words written by the playwright manifest the actions that constitute the plot in the traditional theatre. Traditionally the playwright establishes a situation on stage, disrupts it by placing forces of conflict in opposition, and then usually resolves that conflict. In short, he seeks to arouse the expectations of an audience and then to fulfill them.

Playwrights depend upon other theatre artists to bring their work to life. A director or a producer must select the script; he must find some qualities in the script that make him eager to stage it. Actors present the script to the audience during the production and thus can distort, illuminate, or expand the playwright's intentions. Acting styles have special importance if the playwright attempts innovative writing. Several playwrights have had poor productions of their scripts and have seen later productions vindicate their work. The Russian playwright Anton Chekhov's *The Seagull* offers a classic example. *The Seagull* opened on October 17, 1896, at the Alexandrinsky Theatre in St. Petersburg, was performed by an underrehearsed and uninterested cast whose old-fashioned style clashed with Chekhov's quiet naturalism, and was presented to an audience who expected broad comedy and soon suspected they were being made fools of. The play's failure drove Chekhov from the theatre by the end of the second act; he soon after swore never to write again for the theatre. But a representative of the newly formed and avant-garde Moscow Art Theatre, Nemirovich-Danchenko, prevailed upon him, promising lengthy discussion and equally lengthy rehearsals led by Konstantin Stanislavski, and Chekhov agreed to a second production. On December 17, 1898, the Moscow Art Theatre scored a tremendous and complete success, establishing the theatre, Stanislavski, and Chekhov as the leaders of the Russian theatre.

The innovative playwright depends upon his audience, whose expectations may completely differ from his intentions. Theatre artists and critics now consider *Waiting for Godot* a modern masterpiece, indeed, a key script for the Theatre of the Absurd, but audiences rejected its first production in the United States. Subsequent productions established the script, but only after presentation to audiences capable of perceiving its merit.

FIGURE 2-1. *Anton Chekhov, seated center, reads his script,* The Seagull, *to the members of the Moscow Art Theatre in preparation for rehearsals in 1898.*

The Playwright's Artistic Alternatives and Restrictions

The playwright writes words his audience may never see; actors transmit his words to the audience, hence the uniqueness of writing for the stage compared to literary forms that the public receives via the printed page. The playwright writes a blueprint for a series of actions and transactions, showing rather than describing a set of human relationships and actions. In this regard, the playwright enjoys the vitality of living production as an advantage to his work, but this vitality may be crippled by the modification of his work by other theatre artists. The novelist or the poet, on the other hand, although he must deal with editors, produces his work in solitude; he rarely has anyone else to blame for failure or anything else with whom to share his success.

Writing for the stage presupposes a deep and profound knowledge of the theatre in actual production. With rare exceptions, most of the great playwrights first worked as production personnel, often as actors, before they began to create scripts. Literary values and theatrical values, although related, often differ sharply. Some playwrights, such as Shakespeare, have succeeded on both fronts.

Twenty-five centuries of playwriting have seen a bewildering number of dramatic styles, genres, isms, and intentions come and go for greater or lesser amounts of time. We seem now to have arrived at a theatrical eclecticism in which the playwright may create in any of a vast number of styles, dependent only upon his own talent and preferences. Scholars have attempted to categorize this multitude of dramatic types and describe the stylistic alternatives that the playwright faces.

TYPES OF DRAMA

Perhaps the widest division of dramatic types lies between the representational and the presentational, a distinction that has enjoyed long usage. Representational theatre is the more common of the two, using logical cause and effect in the plot and psychologically credible characterizations. Representational theatre and realistic theatre correlate in many ways: representational theatre seeks to give the audience the illusion that the events, locales, and characters in a production are real. Ideally the audience willingly suspends its disbelief. No one actually considers the events on a stage, no matter how realistically staged and acted, to be actual life events. One may, however, become so engrossed in the action upon the stage that he loses conscious awareness of his surroundings. The representational theatre often elicits such a response. But representational theatre offers an illusion, not to be confused with actual events; the audience becomes emotionally involved with the events on stage up to but not beyond an unacceptable response. If a person were to grow to maturity with no concept of the theatre whatsoever and then attend a play, his response might well be inappropriate. Such is the case in the early American script *The Contrast,* by Royall Tyler, in which the simpleminded and theatrically naive Jonathan is taken to a New York theatre. Having no awareness of theatre, he assumes that when the show started "they lifted up a great green cloth and let us look right into the next neighbor's house," wondering if many houses in New York were so constructed. Similarly a somewhat untrustworthy story has it that a second-rate Shakespearean company once presented *Romeo and Juliet* in a Colorado mining camp to a totally inexperienced audience of sturdy mountain men. All went well till Romeo began to commit suicide, at which point the miners stopped the show, woke up Juliet, dragged a startled Friar Laurence from backstage to remarry them, and celebrated uproari-

29

ously for the next three days. The company eventually escaped to more sophisticated engagements.

Recent outstanding examples of representational drama include *Who's Afraid of Virginia Woolf?*, *That Championship Season, And Miss Reardon Drinks a Little,* and the revivals of *Sherlock Holmes* and *Front Page.* In such productions, the actors traditionally employ the convention of the "fourth wall," in that they perform as though unaware of the audience and as though a fourth wall completed the setting, dividing them from the audience. The actors, of course, listen very carefully to audience reaction, diagnosing and analyzing each audience's specific response.

The presentational theatre, on the other hand, makes no attempt to disguise the onstage action; the cast deals directly with the audience in a face-to-face confrontation. Most musical comedy offers obvious presentationalism; the singers come down center, look directly at the audience, and perform without any attempt at representationalism. Opera seems almost invariably presentational, as do many of the works of Bertolt Brecht, Thornton Wilder, and assorted playwrights of the Theatre of the Absurd.

The Skin of Our Teeth by Thornton Wilder offers presentationalism at its most obvious. The first act is set in New Jersey, and the protagonist, Mr. Antrobus, is busy at the office inventing the alphabet, discovering that ten tens equal one hundred, and inventing the wheel. Purposeful anachronisms abound; the house is typically suburban, complete to a framed sampler reading "God Bless This Home." One of the family's sons is clearly Cain from the Old Testament. The family has two pets, a dinosaur and a mammoth. The pets freeze as the Ice Age strikes, pushing before it assorted refugees; the blind Homer, the Three Graces, and so on. At the end of the first act, the maid, Sabina (from the Sabine women), asks the audience to pass up their chairs and programs for the fire in order that the cast may survive. This script has had innumerable productions, often with great success; the author received the Pulitzer Prize for drama in

1943 for this script. Certainly it presents a truthful depiction of human existence; it never intends to present a realistic one.

Representationalism versus presentationalism does not suggest a right and wrong way to create theatre but instead offers two distinct approaches to the theatrical event, determined by the form of the script and the intentions of the producing agency. Some scripts combine elements of both; some tend one way or the other. Shakespeare's work, for example, may suggest either approach to the director and the actors. Considering a soliloquy, does one present it presentationally to the audience or representationally as though the actor were thinking aloud? Clearly no correct answer exists in all cases, but the director and the actors must come to a clear decision on the matter.

GENERIC CLASSIFICATIONS

Critics and analysts, having studied the drama over the past twenty-five centuries, have evolved a series of terms for the broad divisions and categories that they perceive within the drama. Such attempts to pigeonhole must inevitably meet ultimate failure. Even in the biological sciences, the division of living forms into animal and vegetable seems extremely simple, yet some forms of bacteria continue to defy biological classification. Various subatomic particles cause comparable confusion as physicists attempt to categorize them as matter or energy. Even the distinction between life and death has recently stimulated several court cases.

So, too, scripts defy ultimate categorization. In the final analysis, each script constitutes its own separate form, unique unto itself. Nevertheless, many scripts reveal apparently comparable intentions by the playwrights, hence the usefulness of generic classification such as tragedy, melodrama, comedy, and farce. Certainly a great deal of today's abundant, experimental, avant-garde theatre does

31

not fit the traditional classifications, but the theatregoer will find that most does indeed fall into one of these four basic generic types. Speculation upon the playwright's intention usually associated with each of these forms can lead to an increased capacity to deal with modern experiments in dramatic form as well.

TRAGEDY AND MELODRAMA

As suggested in Chapter One, tragedy seeks to exalt the human spirit. The tragic playwright often seeks this response by revealing a central character in the direst and most serious of dilemmas, beset by forces or agencies that eventually defeat him. Melodrama similarly places its central character(s) in awful circumstances, the classic example being the heroine tied to the train tracks while the hero races to the rescue. What we commonly call melodrama usually achieves a satisfactory resolution: the hero releases the heroine just in the nick of time, defeats the villain once and for all, and usually marries the heroine. But no one arrives to save Oedipus or Hamlet; they meet their defeats and sufferings head on.

To determine the essential distinction between tragedy and melodrama, one must examine the events at the resolution of the basic conflict presented by the playwright. Presupposing a serious treatment of the subject matter in each and a central character or characters faced with substantial dangers, melodrama tends to excite the audience by the sequence of events and satisfy them by the eventual success of the "good guys." Tragedy seeks to engross the audience in the tightening circle of adversity surrounding the hero and satisfies them by the depiction of a human being transcending the fate that destroys him. Melodrama often proves the more exciting of the two genres (what will happen next?), whereas tragedy usually offers more profound insights (how can the hero transcend this destruction?). Righteousness triumphs in melodrama, allowing the playwright to reveal his cleverness in arranging a plot and portraying the world as it ought to be. The protagonist triumphs by his perception in tragedy, allowing the playwright to reveal his comprehension of humanity and a portrayal of the world as it is. Put another way, melodrama suggests that man can fight adversity; tragedy proposes that man can transcend it.

Yet another aspect of the distinction between melodrama and tragedy lies in the nature of the protagonists and their capacity to perceive. A good many melodramas of the purest type have animals as the central character; Lassie, Rin Tin Tin, Black Beauty, and a host of Disney protagonists, both live and animated. Admittedly, a few stage plays contain an animal as a central character for obvious reasons. Audiences have found watching an animal's survival of adversity quite exciting and will watch Lassie's lonely trek across the moors or Rin Tin Tin's heroics with great satisfaction. But no such animal can emerge as the protagonist of a tragedy; we do not attribute the necessary characteristics of abstract thought and capacity to transcend defeat to animals. An animal can suffer, to be sure, but not to the mental and spiritual degree for which a human being has capacity. Thus the inevitable death of a bull in an arena will excite some and stimulate pathos in others, but the bull in humanity's possibly prejudicial opinion lacks the perceptual qualities for tragic stature.

The distinctions presented thus far describe tragedy and melodrama in their purest forms. Playwrights rarely cooperate so neatly with such pigeonholing of their work. Whereas tragedy as a distinct form began in the fifth century b.c., melodrama as a distinct literary genre originated at the turn of the nineteenth century, even though melodramatic elements have appeared from the very beginnings of the theatre. The student may avoid some confusion with regard to these two forms if he will consider tragedy and melodrama not as separate categories but rather as each end of a spectrum with specific scripts tending more or less

33

toward one end or the other of the scale. Such pseudoscientism will not relieve the reader (nor, as we will see later, the producers) of their interpretive responsibilities but may clarify the relationship between intentions. Thus, when faced with a script such as Arthur Miller's *Death of a Salesman,* one need not expend great amounts of energy and time trying to classify it as either a tragedy or a melodrama but may agree with the critic Brooks Atkinson, who suggested that this play "reached the foothills of tragedy." One may similarly consider *The Glass Menagerie, After the Fall,* and a host of modern, serious scripts that obviously supersede melodrama but fail to achieve tragic grandeur. Modern melodrama—such as *Sleuth, Wait Until Dark,* and the detective, hospital, or Western television series—will cause less difficulty.

Since its origins, critics have considered melodrama a lesser literary form than tragedy. Here the sharp distinction between the literary and the theatrical forms comes into sharp focus. In the fourth century B.C., Aristotle, speaking specifically of tragedy, suggested in his *Poetics* six elements of the theatre;

1. Plot, or the arrangement of events within the script.
2. Character, the representing of the personalities in action.
3. Thought, or the ideas contained within the script, related to rhetoric.
4. Diction, the expressive use of language.
5. Music, the accompaniment to Greek production.
6. Spectacle, the visual elements of production.

This scheme of analysis, which still has considerable value to the script analyst, will further reveal distinctions between melodrama and tragedy if one applies each element to prototype scripts. Melodrama, for example, tends to concern itself more with plot and spectacle and less with thought or idea than does tragedy. One might propose man as a creature of hope and therefore more attracted to melodrama, with its ordered good and evil and the hope of escaping the clutches of adversity, than to the more complex tragic concept of surviving one's fate. Certainly melodrama has been far more commercially successful in the history of theatre, but tragedy has been more enduring. Literary critics especially have found the enduring qualities of tragedy of far more worth than the temporary values of theatrical melodrama. Audiences have more often sought excitement than profundity.

Critics have devised a variety of terms to describe serious drama other than tragedy. Italian Renaissance scholars, for example, used *tragicomedy* to describe scripts they considered a mixture of tragedy and comedy, characterized by aristocratic characters in a script with a happy ending or a script in which various death threats were happily avoided. Another term, *drame,* came from the French to characterize contemporary plays of serious intent. Students will still encounter both terms with some frequency.

COMEDY AND FARCE

Just as critics have considered melodrama somehow inferior to tragedy, they have similarly considered comic forms of less substance than serious drama. Seemingly, if a playwright wants serious consideration, he must write serious drama. Yet the comic forms frequently hold greater appeal for audiences.

The student may further consider that the comic theatre in the majority of societies, from the primitive to the more complex, usually develops and emerges only after the serious drama has arrived and florished. Exceptions exist, of course, but theatre historians find such a sequence common. Does this sequence imply a society can accept the seemingly inconsequential comic theatre only after it has satisfied more serious concerns? Or that the society must develop more completely before it can perceive humor with

35

regard to itself? Or that audiences, although they may flock to the humorous, do not hold comedy in as high regard as the seemingly more substantial serious drama?

Once again, no definitive answer presents itself, but the student need not decry the weakness of intellectual analysis. Let him rather celebrate the richness of human endeavor that transcends categorization. Seeming to seek merely to amuse (as if diversion in the modern world needed justification), comedy does not evade the substantial in life; rather it approaches our existence from a different point of view than that of tragedy and the serious forms. Some nameless theoretician has pointed out that life is a tragedy for those who feel and a comedy for those who think.

Perhaps the most overtly purposeful comic form is that of satire, comedy that uses irony, sarcasm, and ridicule to expose, denounce, or deride human vice and folly. Such comic writing in general, often savage in its attack, hardly avoids matters of consequence and more often addresses them quite directly. Examples of satire abound from Aristophanes in fifth-century Greece through Molière in seventeenth-century France to Mark Twain in the last century to the present-day Al Capp's "Li'l Abner" and Gary Trudeau's comic strip, "Doonesbury." Such a comic form seeks to correct society and the ills thereof by ridiculing the undesirable aspects of it.

At the opposite end of the comic scale lies farce, that comic form that seeks only to amuse with no conscious function beyond evoking laughter. This comic form uses slapstick, prat falls, pies in the face, chase scenes, seltzer bottles, bladders, and the like. Modern examples would include the Charlie Chaplin films, the Three Stooges, burlesque comedy, and the frequently revived works of George Feydeau (1862–1921). To some critics, farce represents the least substantial of all comic forms, apparently divorced entirely from thought or idea. But other critics find much merit in some farces, audiences often find them delightful, and theatre artists find the production of successful farce calls for creativity of the highest order.

The term *comedy,* although referring to the totality of comic forms, refers particularly to the middle ground between satire, with its savagery, and farce, with its mindlessness. Comedy in this sense corresponds to the great bulk of serious drama lying between tragedy and melodrama; it employs thought as an element very definitely, but it does not call attention to the fact. Much of the situation comedy on television, for example, does indeed present a point of view, as in the "Mary Tyler Moore Show," "Happy Days," "Good Times," "M.A.S.H.," and the like, but that point of view is not hammered home so blatantly as in satire. Similarly, the comic strip "Charlie Brown" has much to say of value about human relationships, but Charles Schultz offers the "message" without sermonizing. The unequalled response to this comic strip by both children and adults suggests an appeal of substantial significance.

Comedy in general, from satire to farce, invariably involves the sudden collision of two planes of thought in a suddenly revealed combination. The "punch line" of an anecdote triggers the listener's grasp of this new relationship. Cartoons in popular magazines most frequently reveal the fundamentals of such collisions as a basis for comedy. Puns and spoonerisms similarly wrench words from one context into another, and the audience's perception of the new relationship leads to laughter. If, of course, the audience does not recognize the collision, if they "don't get it," frustration results, but not laughter or smiles. Because comedy frequently depends upon the local and the topical for effect, classical comedy frequently leaves the modern reader quite cold. Aristophanes's brilliant satires on the administration of the political leader of Athens, Cleon, require a considerable background in Athenian history, and his outrageous, often obscene puns simply cannot be translated from one language to another. So, too, Shakespeare's punning on the words *heart* and *hart* or his treatments of the term *equivocation* make very little sense to the modern reader; they depended upon a specific set of circumstances long since gone. That so much of his writing does still appeal strongly to modern readers and audiences reveals his universality and avoidance of the trivial.

In examinations of this generic division of drama, the critical preference for tragedy and satire seems to stem from their overt use of the element of thought; ideas of substance attract literary respectability. *Drame* and comedy in the narrower sense, although acceptable, lack the stature of tragedy and satire; they require less conscious mental effort on the part of the audience. Farce and melodrama do not often stimulate mental activity on the audience's part; they have often been doomed by the intelligentsia as lesser forms while being praised by the mass audiences without whom the theatre cannot survive.

Viewed from yet another angle, these six generic terms perhaps indicate six methods of viewing a specific human action, human action in general, or existence in general, varying from the spiritual optimism of tragedy to the raucous irreverence of farce. Thus a single dramatic theme or situation can, should the playwright choose, be treated in any of these ways. Consider the popular subject of adultery, treated as tragedy in *Othello;* as comedy in *Measure for Measure;* as satire in Joseph Orton's *What the Butler Saw;* as *drame* in *Tea and Sympathy, A Streetcar Named Desire, Desire Under the Elms,* and *The Crucible;* as farce in most of the scripts by Feydeau, such as *A Flea in Her Ear;* and as melodrama daily in the television soap operas. But if tragedy and satire reveal humanity most thoughtfully, farce and melodrama suggest a world in which good triumphs over evil and in which repression and frustration scarcely exist. *Drame* and comedy, combining the most popular of both extremes, have combined critical worth and popular appeal and thus have succeeded most consistently over the long history of the theatre.

Obviously, playwrights do not merely select one of these six genres and begin to write. In the modern drama they often combine elements in varying degrees of all dramatic forms, selecting those elements that seem to them most appropriate to their specific intentions. Shakespeare, for example, mixes the serious and the comic in *Hamlet,* intensifying each by counterpointing it against the other. Just as graphic artists use highlight and shadow to depict a three-dimensional form, playwrights commonly perceive life as a mixture of the serious and the comic; they thus use both approaches in depicting human existence upon the stage.

Requisites for Excellence in Playwriting

Like any other writer, the playwright must have, above all, a strong urge to write. This requirement eliminates many persons who want to be writers, something quite distinct from wanting to write. The writer does not spend, contrary to popular opinion, most of his time at cocktail parties given by his publishers or in cashing royalty checks. Rather he spends his time alone trying to get his ideas and words together in acceptable form. Clear writing results from hard work.

Perseverance thus emerges as a primary quality for the writer, dogged persistence and stamina that see him through the creation, revisions, and rewriting of his work. He also needs sheer perceptiveness, the ability to see the world around him with a profound penetration and understanding, usually leading him to a somewhat sympathetic view of the human circumstance. Obviously, as words constitute the primary means of transmission, the writer engages in a lifelong study, formal or informal, of language.

Akin to perception, the playwright must depict characters

39

in action to elicit an appropriate response from an audience. Such a task implies profound understanding of individuals of all sorts; the varieties of human interaction, motivation, and purpose; and the nature of groups, including audiences. Stated bluntly, the task seems beyond human ability; playwrights seek the ideal of total understanding of humanity.

Any artist sets out to achieve a self-created aesthetic level. The writer usually goes through lengthy polishing of his manuscript, altering and changing and often rejecting. The writer must have that rare combination of ability, humility, and courage to eliminate from his work whatever fails to attain his personal standards; he must select ruthlessly to retain the valuable. As Hemingway put it, "the most essential gift for a good writer is a built-in, shock-proof shit detector. This is the writer's radar and all great writers have had it." The writer thus functions as a critic in action for his own work.

A theatrical background seems essential for the successful playwright. A few exceptions notwithstanding, writing for so specialized a field as the theatre demands intimate awareness of the unique qualities of live performance. Mere exposure or experience seldom suffices; the playwright must deeply understand the theatrical interaction before he can hope to create it successfully.

Insofar as higher education can lead to an overview of humanity, the playwright can benefit from formal study. Clearly many excellent playwrights have had no formal education and have drawn upon their own perceptual genius and solitary study. Most playwrights read plays to gain an appreciation of other playwrights' techniques and an awareness of their vision of reality.

The writer gains something else, usually called craft, from the very act of writing, a sort of "paying one's dues" or the accumulation of experience and insight into one's art. All artists seem to serve comparable apprenticeships. Eventually the writer emerges with a better sense of what he can

40

do and how he can do it. A personal style emerges, born out of internal preference and external reinforcement.

Finally, just as the novelist considers potential markets for his work, the playwright must keep in close touch with all possible producing agencies and all theatrical movements of his time. The beginning playwright should especially concern himself with the various playwriting contests, as they often offer him production opportunity. The playwright must see his work staged by a cast before an audience if he writes for the theatre.

The Playwright's Contemporary Situation

At the present time, very few playwrights earn a living only by writing; most need supplemental income. Television and film writing offer greater opportunities and financial security for the writer. Broadway productions have declined in number in recent years, and although other opportunities for the playwright have increased somewhat, financial reward is rarely commensurate with the requisite effort.

In spite of these unfortunate circumstances, more and more playwrights appear, both vocationally and avocationally. Colleges and universities have seen increasing demand for playwriting courses; production opportunities increase in studio and main-stage theatres. Playwrights assume there is room at the top for excellence and continue to turn out scripts in great numbers. The recent increase in leisure time, wide exposure to the dramatic media of all sorts, and a seeming increase in a personal need to express one's point of view in part account for this activity.

Very few playwrights achieve excellence; the excellent by definition rarely occurs in any human endeavor. For the fortunate and persevering few who do receive early reinforcement for their work, submitting scripts to theatrical agents for possible professional production seems the major hurdle. If one can convince an agent of his work's commercial marketability, the agent then circulates the script among potential producers. At this point, commercial considerations supersede aesthetics; the enormous sums of money required for professional production tend to make investors cautious. Estimates of the odds against commercial success in New York City vary, but roughly eight productions out of nine fail to break even financially.

Yet the successful playwright can reap enormous rewards. Income not only from Broadway productions but from television series, motion-picture rights, publication of the scripts, and royalties from other productions, professional and amateur, all contribute.

The playwright with a completed script must find production possibilities for his script. Having concerned himself with the aesthetics of writing the script, he must then consider his work as a commodity for the market and find somewhere to sell it, or at least to see it on stage. If the playwright does not envision the Broadway stage as his only avenue for exposure, several possibilities exist. Foremost among them are his own personal contacts in the theatrical profession. His acquaintances will more likely read and assess his work than will relative strangers. The playwright should also own copies of such publications as *The Writers' Yearbook* and *Simon's Directory of Theatrical Materials, Services, and Information,* both of which include lists of potential outlets. The two leading script publishers—Samuel French, Inc., and Dramatists Play Service, Inc.—have readers to examine new scripts. A good many college and university theatre departments solicit new scripts for possible production. Finally, he may submit his work directly to a play agent, many of whom are listed in *Simon's Directory,* but such agents, when dealing with a playwright unknown to them, prefer a letter describing the script rather than the completed manuscript itself. For college and university students, the American College Theatre Festival, held each year, actively solicits new scripts for regional and national competitions and offers substantial prizes for winning scripts produced by colleges or universities. Further details are available from the American Theatre Association.

The playwright should also investigate the professional organization for playwrights, the Dramatists Guild, Inc., a corporate member of the Authors League of America, Inc. Throughout the long history of this group, they have organized and fought valiantly for the rights of American authors and have scored significant successes in such matters as copyright laws, sales of film rights, income averaging for tax purposes, and negotiations with producers.

Such matters may seem far removed from the artist's aesthetic considerations and out of place in such a discussion, but the artist has the right to seek financial security from his work. Art is the vocation of the artist, and he frequently must consider such pragmatic matters. If he writes purely out of commercial considerations, he will probably reduce his aesthetic potential, and if he seeks only fame, he will find it elusive. The playwright creates in solitude. If he can satisfy himself that what he has created represents his best possible work, he achieves an undeniable satisfaction. Commercial concerns follow, perhaps as a secondary consideration, but one of monumental significance.

Artists who receive continual rejection do not long remain artists. The starving painter in his wretched garret may be a romantic figure, but he will not continue to starve in most cases; he will either die or seek income elsewhere. Economics thus enters into every art field. The purist may consider financial concerns a corruption of aesthetics, but he will also find them inescapable.

Creative Procedures for the Playwright

Because the playwright, unlike other theatrical artists, works alone—at least at first—and does not in the early

43

stages have significant interaction with the other artists, he enjoys far greater freedom in approaching his work. Until he submits his final draft to a producer, he can work in whatever way he prefers. Nevertheless most playwrights have found systematic procedures most productive, and the following steps typify most writers' working methods.

First, the playwright must have both the general creative urge and the specific stimulation to write a particular work. For the playwright this urge often grows out of experiential reinforcement in the theatre, usually as a participant. Frequently the playwright progressed through acting to directing or producing plays before beginning to create his own scripts. Generally one will find early theatrical experiences of this sort in playwrights' biographies (Aeschylus, Plautus, Shakespeare, Jonson, Sheridan, Brecht, Molière, O'Neill, and so on) and will further find that the playwright typically creates very little of substance until he has reached an artistic, social, and theatrical maturity of vision or until he has accumulated sufficient personal resources upon which to draw. Again, a few exceptions occur.

As for the stimulation of a specific script, no clear-cut pattern emerges as to why the playwright pursues a particular concept to its completion. As stated in Chapter One, the artwork's function and the artist's intention may involve entertainment, edification, or exaltation of the human spirit, or more likely a combination of those three purposes. Specific stimulation for a script may arise from a person or character, an incident or circumstance, from an idea, thought, or message, or even from a specific locale. These may spur the playwright into action. Perhaps simply that the creative urge does happen is more important than how it happens. Writers—indeed, all artists—speak of "drying up," failing for one reason or the other to find the necessary creative stimulation. They find various means of combating this problem.

Full-fledged works do not often flash into the minds of artists, and playwrights offer no exception. Following the

44

first stage, the creative urge, comes the execution of the script. At this point, the unwary novice begins writing dialogue, usually without a clear concept of where the action may lead and without careful character delineations, much as an unwise term paper writer begins the actual writing before planning the overall structure.

Similarly the playwright usually does well to continue fleshing out his original concept, accumulating more and more material for his script before beginning. Usually he plots out the rough sequence of events, called a *scenario*. It is simple at first, but growing more and more detailed and comprehensive as he continues polishing. This scenario parallels outlining a speech or a paper. The writer preplans and structures the event as a whole before dealing with the details and minutiae along the way. When assured that he has completed this step to the best of his ability, he then writes a first rough draft of the complete work.

Just as in term paper writing, he may find his scenario unsatisfactory, and he may have to go back to earlier stages of the script's development to solve hitherto unforeseen problems. If successful, he will eventually complete a first draft of the script.

He then enters the third stage of playwriting, that of revision. Many playwrights have suggested that plays are not written but rewritten. Most writers agree.

Revising a script seldom seems as exciting as writing the scenarios and the first draft, but this step frequently determines the script's eventual success or failure. Like any artist, the playwright at this stage predicts audience response to his work. He seeks to perfect his work according to his intentions till he can improve it no more. Just as intentions, techniques, and talents of playwrights vary widely, so do the number and extent of revisions vary, even in the work of one author. Hopefully he eventually completes a final draft, which he or his agent submits to producing agencies. Even then, however, the playwright's work may continue. Ideally he should attend some rehearsals and confer frequently with the production's director. The script slowly becomes a play, how successfully depends upon the playwright's prophetic skills, assuming competent directing and acting. Almost inevitably he will see in rehearsal further possible improvements. He continues, in effect, to prophesy, but he has more evidence now. He sees the play rather than his printed words, he hears his lines instead of reading them to himself, and he has the responses of the producing company to assist him and to extend his basis for evaluation.

As production nears, the script takes its semifinal form before presentation to an audience. The most important agency of all, the audience, then tests all the previous predictions. Playwrights and directors must examine audience responses most carefully at this point. In the commercial theatre, most plays open either on the road (that is, outside New York) or to preview audiences before their official opening so that playwrights and directors can, if necessary, make further adjustments. In repertory situations and sometimes in long-run circumstances, further changes can be made after the show has opened.

Eventually all the theatre artists decide that they have done the best they can under the circumstances. The script has jelled; it has set; the playwright has completed his task. Only one step remains possible, the publication of the script. The playwright must once again prepare a clean copy of his work, submit it to the publishers, and check the galley proofs. As mentioned earlier, film and television producers' versions may require another version, but in that case the playwright writes for a different medium, or another writer revises the original script for that medium.

Although the four stages of conception, execution, revision, and publication describe the creative procedures of a good many playwrights, the actuality of creation can vary tremendously. Bursts of creative inspiration occur frequently in the arts, and artists employ any means helpful to the creative process. Being an art, theatre is not governed by any set of laws or regulations yet discovered.

46

Although plays rarely leap into a playwright's mind all at once, in some cases they do. Eugene O'Neill awoke one morning with a new play "fully in mind," even to the title, and in less than a month he had finished the enduring *Ah, Wilderness!* If legend is to be believed, Arthur Miller's *Death of a Salesman,* Edward Albee's *Zoo Story,* George Farquhar's *The Recruiting Officer,* John Osborne's *Look Back in Anger,* and several of Noel Coward's scripts had similar births.

Very few people care how an artist creates or how long it takes him; they are concerned only with the finished work. Usually, however, craftsmanship and inspiration combine in the successful creative process in any of the arts.

Evaluating the Playwright's Contribution

Because a play in production amalgamates the artistic efforts of many people, to separate one element, the script, from the total effect requires considerable theatrical sophistication and experience. Each element of production modifies and affects every other element, leading to an interdependency of effort and making evaluation of anything less than the produced play's total effect most difficult. If a scene or a speech plays especially well in production, for example, to what degree does one credit the playwright for writing a good speech or the actor for delivering it well? Ideally the playwright has written a speech that an actor can deliver well, and both share the credit.

Seemingly one can distinguish the playwright's contributions more easily than those of the other theatre artists because his work exists in a uniquely separate form, the script. But not many playgoers read the script of a play that they plan to see. Nor does reading a script from the printed page always clearly reveal the playwright's intention, especially to the newcomer to the theatre. Presupposing an ex-

47

cellent production, some scripts read better than they play in production, just as some scripts play better than they read. Thus the script reader must envision a production in his mind; he must cast, set, direct, light, and costume the script in his mind's eye, drawing upon his own theatrical experience and taste. Experienced professionals encounter considerable difficulty in reading scripts and predicting success or failure, and theatrical neophytes usually encounter considerable frustration in this regard. Conversely, if one evaluates the playwright's work from a production, he must dissect an interrelated, organic, dynamic entity; if he reads the script, he must conjure up all the production elements.

Further complicating the matter, strong productions of weak scripts occur, as do weak productions of strong scripts. Recently one of the world's outstanding professional companies contracted with an established playwright to produce one of his new scripts. The writing did not go well for assorted reasons; audiences found the eventual script as produced almost totally incomprehensible; the playwright's intentions did not reach the audience, nor could any imaginable production techniques short of massive cutting and rewriting clarify the issues. Nevertheless, the company had advertised the production, sold tickets, rehearsed the show, built scenery, and so on. The production company gave the script a strong production, but the script's undeniable weaknesses doomed the entire venture. Because the company presents shows in repertory, they could survive this failure, which ran a short time to ever-decreasing audiences and eventually passed into theatrical limbo. The playwright and company went on separately to better things.

One may encounter a production of a dramatic masterpiece by a company unprepared financially, aesthetically, technically, or spiritually to perform a work of such scope. Perhaps the most common instance of this sort occurs when student groups attempt scripts clearly beyond their potential. A ludicrous example might be a junior high school

speech class doing *Hamlet* or *Oedipus Rex* for public performance; few students at that stage of development can even
attempt either protagonist. Perhaps such an experience
would benefit the performers; conceivably such a production might even have value to a young audience who had
never seen or read either script. But one ought not to confuse educational and aesthetic values. Indeed, because the
intentions of educational theatre emerge as somewhat distinct from those of the commercial theatre, critics should
probably apply an equally distinct basis for evaluation. In
public performance, however, as opposed to class work and
studio work, the audience expects much the same rewards
for attendance as they do in the commercial theatre. They
expend time and effort to attend, and the producing
agency should not deny its responsibility to them.

Evaluators must therefore carefully delineate the playwright's contribution in light of its dependency upon the
production and the production's dependency upon what
the playwright has created, and if the theatregoer intends
such evaluation, he must attempt such division.

Having distinguished the playwright's contribution, the
audience member then responds to it. On the most fundamental level, he either liked or did not like the play
and/or the script, but the thoughtful viewer will seek to discover his basis for preference. The relative newcomer to
theatregoing may at first use the deceptively simple question pattern originated by Goethe in evaluating art forms of
all types:

1. What was the artist trying to do?
2. How well did he do it?
3. Was it worth doing?

So apparently obvious an approach does not offer auto-
matic nor ultimate insight but will supply the modicum of
form requisite to analysis and discussion. Nor does this ap-

49

proach negate the subjective in criticism and evaluation, although it can help one to avoid some of the more common pitfalls of artistic evaluation.

The first question seeks the playwright's intention: What was the artist trying to do to his audience? What effect did he seek to have on those who experienced his work? If the audience member does not perceive the playwright's purpose, his analysis and evaluation suffer. Here again background resources from theatregoing, script reading, and other appropriate experiences enrich perception; the audience member/critic must first of all know what options and theatrical potentials the playwright had.

One must remember, of course, that historians often refer to the "intentional fallacy," suggesting that no one can indeed know the motivations of another. Suggesting that an artist's intentions (what was he trying to do?) offer a means of evaluating an artwork leads us to the brink of intentional fallacy, suggesting that we can never know the artist's intentions, even if he himself has articulated them. Some critics feel that Bertolt Brecht, for example, wrote both clearly and at length about the effects he sought as a dramatist, but the same critics sometimes suggest that his scripts have very little to do with his theories. As one scholar recently put it, "Brecht's theories are what he thought he thought about when he thought about writing plays."

But as Cyrano de Bergerac says, "A man does not fight merely to win." Very likely it is impossible to know completely the motivations and aspirations of another human being, especially with regard to so complex a matter as the production of art. Goethe's concept of edification, entertainment, and exaltation offer only three sweeping generalizations about artistic motivation; the artist's personal circumstances complicate matters much more.

So why bother? Because the *process* of speculating upon the artist's intentions will very often illuminate the artwork in the mind of the viewer, depending upon his imagination, experience, and perception. By addressing himself to the problem of intention, the viewer finds himself speculating upon the artist's options and alternatives; the process usually leads to a deeper understanding and hence appreciation. By meeting the artist half way, the viewer opens himself to far richer insights.

Thus the audience member in the theatre may ask whether the playwright sought to entertain the audience, to edify it, or to exalt the human spirit. These categories overlap, as do Goethe's three questions. Nevertheless the playwright's intended effect gives us a beginning: In what way did he seek to affect his audience? To suggest that if an artist sought one effect critics ought not to condemn him for not achieving another effect may seem obvious, but one often encounters such criticism. One should not criticize a television situation comedy for not exalting the human spirit; the producer probably sought only to entertain or amuse. Nor does one especially need to feel disappointed if a musical comedy does not contain much edification for the onlooker; the production probably intended diversion and entertainment. Nor does a Greek tragedy amuse in the usual sense; the playwright sought to do more than merely titillate. Given the wide variety and spectrum of theatrical possibilities, all shows cannot offer all things to all people; audience tastes and predilections vary so widely that only a part of the total output of the theatre can satisfy each audience member. Human preference varies of necessity in all other art forms, in politics, religion, clothing, food, and so on. All the more reason, perhaps, for the audience member to try to find something out about a production ahead of time rather than trusting to luck, but he should also seek new experiences to widen his personal as well as his theatrical scope.

The second question—How well did the artist accomplish his aims?—again involves subjective preferences. One can argue indefinitely whether a show was well done or not, but no one can argue whether or not a specific audience member liked it or not. However, when a viewer suggests

51

that an artwork is bad *because* he doesn't like it or that it is good *because* he likes it, he puts himself on dangerous ground. Such presumptuous egoism suggests ultimate insight, rarely attainable.

But if the artist sought to entertain and the onlooker found the experience disagreeable to watch, the transaction between the artist and the recipient failed. This failure can originate on either side of the art work. If the audience member, for instance, was mugged and robbed on the way into the theatre, he may well be incapable of being entertained. But if the audience member approached the work openly, if he sought entertainment and didn't find it, one must look elsewhere for the problem.

Similarly, if the audience member expects one thing and finds another, the artist–recipient interaction often breaks down. Just as the student of old masters' painting may be confused by modern art, the traditionalist in the theatre will find only frustration in viewing many contemporary plays. Just as a Bach fan may reject the atonality of some modern music, the audience member seeking only diversion may react with hostility when the playwright and the company seek other ends. How well the artist accomplished his goals may well be lost if the goals are outside the experience or the preference of the onlooker. This circumstance reveals the interdependence of the first two of Goethe's questions and implies the third.

Whether or not the entire artwork deserved the artist's and the recipient's attention constitutes the third and final value judgment. For example, those who find entertainment frivolous and inconsequential usually seek a loftier goal for art. Others may find edification, especially of the cerebral sort found in didactic drama, inappropriate for art and feel that art should first and foremost give pleasure to the beholder. Some consider depictions of the human spirit the proper concern of other endeavors, such as religion or philosophy, and insist that art and the theatre should not venture into this field. One's personal vision of artistic functions colors his evaluation of any art form, just as one's personal preferences and prejudices modify the reality surrounding him and indeed determine his own universe in his mind's eye.

Thus the breadth and depth of one's world vision permeate his response to art and form the basis for his evaluation of what he experiences. Rather than decrying this subjectivity, the thoughtful student or audience member recognizes it, feeds it into his considerations of an artistic experience, and fully understands that his unique humanity completes the artistic transaction and thereby modifies it. In the playwright–audience interaction, the original work filters through the work of dozens of other theatre artists before reaching the audience, each stage of preparation and rehearsal modifying the eventual production, which is modified further by the individual audience member. In most art forms, almost as much time and energy is spent in discussion as in creation.

Conclusions

The playwright's script represents an intermediary form between his original decision to write and the completed art form, the play in production. Like other artists, the playwright has infinite choice in giving form to his life response; unlike many artists, his work contributes to an art form rather than forming an artistic entity. If all the theatre artists involved succeed in their collaboration, the eventual production can serve the audience in the ways that Goethe outlined, giving them an insight into the human condition in a form unavailable in any other art.

Chapter Three

The Director

*"Later on I came to see that standing in the
middle of the stage and making others do the
work is not the sole qualification for being a
producer [director]."*
—EDWARD GORDON CRAIG, *Woodcuts and
Some Words*

RECENTLY a young director had gone backstage on the
opening night of a high school play under his direction and
then had gone to the lobby to await the play's start. There a
startled student usher confronted him and asked, "Aren't
you the director of this play?" When the director admitted
he was, the student, staring at him in bewilderment, asked,
"Then why aren't you back there *directing* it?"

The question seems more reasonable in retrospect than it
did at the time. Audiences often equate the direction of a
theatrical production with coaching an athletic team or con-
ducting a symphonic orchestra, and they see the coach or
the conductor actually present during the performance,
having visible impact upon the events under way. Although
some directors in educational theatre do indeed remain
backstage during performance, most do not. They have
prepared the cast and crews for the performance and have
placed them under the authority of a stage manager, so the
director finds himself almost superfluous and often retires

to the back of the auditorium to evaluate the performance. In some cases, the director may come backstage during intermissions to speak to the cast or the crew; in emergencies he may go back during the performance.

For the most part, the audience member sees less concrete evidence of the director's contributions than of those of the other theatrical artists. Whereas playwrights and designers present tangible results of their labor, as do theatre architects, and whereas actors present themselves visibly and personally to the audience, the director's efforts seem much more difficult to distinguish, describe, or evaluate.

The director supervises all aesthetic elements of a theatrical production. Modern theatrical production entails a multitude of complexities. Lest the endeavor come to total chaos (a very real danger), a single person must unify the work of others. Someone once called a camel a horse designed by a committee; rarely do artistic endeavors succeed when the final resort is a consensus.

Whereas the modern concept of a theatrical director dates from only a century ago, in almost all the theatrical ages of the past, some individual took charge of production: the playwright, the leading actor, the financial manager of the troupe, or the owner of the theatre. Stock characters and stock scenery may have made production simpler in those days, but as more naturalistic settings and acting came to the theatre and as historical accuracy in costumes, scenery, and lighting followed the technological advances and increasing interest in history in the nineteenth century, the burgeoning complexity of staging a play demanded a central figure of some authority. An uncoached athletic team may win some success, and an unconducted symphonic orchestra may win praise, but efficiency increases and things run much more smoothly under the capable direction of a unifying individual. In the modern theatre, that individual is the director.

The director can give a production the quality of unity otherwise achieved only by coincidence or chance. Ideally he determines his own intention for the production, engages the other artists, and filters their creative work through his own vision, welding all effort into a smooth, cohesive whole. In doing so, he works as a practical prophet, predicting audience responses to particular staging procedures and drawing upon his own experience and creativity, as well as those of his fellow artists. The modern director has rightfully been called a critic in action. During the rehearsals he evaluates and can immediately modify and hopefully improve the overall effort. In some situations, such as in repertory, he may be able to rework a production after it has opened to the public. In many ways, his is the most responsible of theatrical positions. He has often selected the script; cast, hired, rehearsed the actors; approved all the visual elements of scenery, costumes, makeup, and lighting; and in effect overseen the entire production according to his aesthetic vision. In so doing, he uses the artistry of others as his artistic medium, just as a coach uses the skills of others to create something greater than the sum of its parts. Both coaches and directors assume a considerable responsibility, calling for the highest qualities of leadership in the pursuit of excellence.

The Director's Alternatives and Restrictions

The very nature of the modern live theatre offers the director considerable freedom in which to work. He often has the total body of dramatic literature from which to choose, plus available unproduced scripts. In the commercial theatre, the producer usually hires a director to stage a specific script, whereas the educational theatre director, in different fiscal circumstances, has wider choices in script selection. Further, the director can deal with a specific script in a variety of ways or styles. For example, Shakespeare wrote for a specific staging style, but directors have chosen to present his scripts in a remarkable variety of ways; *Macbeth* in Haiti,

FIGURE 3-1. *The director watches carefully as the actors rehearse. Permission from the University of Missouri Department of Speech and Dramatic Art.*

A Midsummer Night's Dream in Texas, *The Merchant of Venice* in the London of 1890, *The Taming of the Shrew* in modern Greenwich Village, and so on. Such experiments do not always succeed, but given the choice of several thousand scripts and hundreds of production styles, the director enjoys almost infinite freedom of choice as he conceives his production.

The restrictions of the live theatre, however, constantly restrain the director. The limitations of stage production, which usually takes place in a relatively small space, prohibit some effects. Although producers can and have successfully staged such spectacles as the chariot race in *Ben Hur,* the effect could not compare to that of the most recent film. Spectacle, a traditional theatrical element, can be achieved far more impressively in a motion picture than on a stage.

58

Shakespearean battle scenes trouble most modern directors for this reason. Whereas an Elizabethan audience with no cinematic background might accept the convention of a few dozen actors representing two armies, modern audiences may find it ludicrous, and even Shakespeare felt the need to apologize for his stage's limitations in the prologue to *Henry V* (see the introductory quotation to Chapter Six). So too, rapid shifts of locale involve expense and difficulty if attempted realistically in the theatre. Again, film offers a more flexible medium for such effects. Most directors in the legitimate theatre forgo the advantages of spectacle in order to work with living actors rather than projected images.

Perhaps most significantly, the limitations of those with whom he works may restrict the director, just as his own limitations do. To the extent that the director brings intelligence, sensitivity, craftsmanship, dedication, creativity, and experience to the production, he will contribute. The same holds true for the other theatre artists. The cooperative effort required in the theatre reveals itself as both an advantage and disadvantage. Just as a skilled athlete may make up for a weaker player on a team, so may one theatre artist assist another, but limits exist and pervasive weaknesses will erode the overall worth of a production.

Finally, the director in the theatre usually works with a smaller budget than the film director, as well as for a lower salary. No amount of money can buy artistic excellence, but because of a smaller potential audience, the living theatre usually cannot invest as much money in production as can electronic or cinematic media.

The Requisites for Excellence in Directing

With the impact of the modern director upon production excellence, artistic success requires a talented and well-trained director. To achieve that success, the director must bring many diverse talents and qualities to his work. Above all, he must have the desire for excellence, as opposed to a willingness to do enough to get by. In educational theatre, one hears the occasional excuses that box-office income does not always determine the success of the program, that local criticism may be laughed off as the work of amateurs, that low audience attendance can be blamed on competing events or on a low local cultural level, or that inexperienced actors prohibit excellence. Similarly, commercial directors curse the theatrical unions, the audiences, the critics, the dearth of playwrights, and the escalating ticket prices. As in most human endeavor, many participants tend to blame outside forces for their failures, yet many directors go far beyond the minimal requirements of direction and achieve productions of substantial merit. Although protestations of seeking excellence are almost universal, the requisite effort appears less commonly, even though, as the Duke of Saxe-Meiningen, one of the first great directors, said a century ago, "There are no excuses in the theatre."

Executive ability becomes a requisite of directorial excellence because the director oversees activities of great variety. Designers bring different problems to productions than do business managers; property crews require a different treatment from understudies; stage lighting problems distinctly differ from costume difficulties; and so on. Supervision and unification of such variant matters call for substantial managerial talents and a capacity to order priorities, delegate responsibility, and cut through detail to the core of the matter. Furthermore the various endeavors frequently develop at different speeds, and unified scheduling is demanded if the show is to open on schedule. One actor may develop at a pace different from another, further complicating rehearsals.

Ultimately all unsolved problems end up on the director's desk. The author recalls a recent production of his for which he asked the property crew to supply two rubber

60

chickens for a sight gag. Search as they might, the crew could find no outlet for rubber chickens in central Missouri. Eventually a friend in St. Louis supplied them from a novelty shop there. Such problems are commonplace in the theatre. If one directs *Inherit the Wind,* one will either decide not to use the organ-grinder's monkey, or one will set about locating a monkey for rent. Working in the theatre frequently offers some unique challenges.

Successful directing demands not only supervision but leadership. Leaders of any sort tend to achieve the degree of respect they deserve. Actors especially need someone watching their work whom they trust and respect. Once secure in that relationship, they can experiment freely in rehearsal, knowing that a sympathetic director can eliminate excesses and misjudgments. Of the volumes written about the qualities of leadership, most apply directly to the stage director.

This leadership quality demands the ability to communicate clearly and efficiently. The director with magnificent but inarticulate conceptions offers little to anyone and succeeds only in frustrating all concerned. Once, watching a college theatre rehearsal, the author heard a young director tell his assembled cast, "The most important thing is . . . the most important thing!" Needless to say, the cast required further details. Even in the commercial theatre, the director functions very much as a teacher, sharing with his fellow artists his conception of a particular production and professing his theatrical philosophy. In educational and amateur theatre, the teaching responsibilities of the director appear more obvious. In a larger sense, the director uses the production, as does the playwright, to instruct or edify an audience.

To achieve his goals, the director must have developed the skills of understanding and analyzing human relations and interaction, both those of the producing company of actors and technicians and those of the human personalities delineated in the script. The director never perfects this talent, of course; a complete understanding of humanity would approximate divinity. Nevertheless the director properly pursues this total understanding, as does any artist, using his complete life experience to illuminate his work. The director's investigation of art in general and theatre scripts in particular exposes him to the vision of many of the leading thinkers and artists of all time. This study can substantially increase his awareness of human action and conditions.

Directors must learn their craft just as a linguist learns a language. Even the mechanics of arranging actors on a stage offers more problems than might at first appear. Interaction between production elements (scenery, costumes, properties, and so on) and actors is of utmost importance. The director must have a sympathetic understanding of the problems of all concerned and the ability to resolve problems and facilitate excellence. Successful directors develop these skills over a period of time, although some seem to have innate talents in this regard.

Finally, and perhaps most important, the director must have imagination. Creativity as the hallmark of the arts requires the artist to sift his experiences, his materials, and his vision and combine them in new expressions; otherwise he only repeats himself. The creation of artworks never before seen, never before experienced, necessarily constitutes the artist's proper pursuit.

Formal training plays an important part in a director's development as it can enhance a latent talent and interest. The director must be a man of the theatre, totally, perhaps even more than the other theatre artists. Ideally he must be familiar with every facet of theatrical production from program-copy layout to the structure of iambic pentameter. The director faces daily an unending series of decisions to make or supervise in every facet of staging, and misjudgment or hesitation can dilute the eventual production.

Most directors begin as actors, often in high school or college. Undergraduates do not often consciously seek directorial careers but rather spend the four-year program working in all facets of theatre. For this reason, undergraduate programs most commonly constitute majors in theatre, whereas at the M.A., M.S., or M.F.A. level, theatre majors specialize in acting, directing, design, management, and so on. Many outstanding modern American directors received their first theatre training in educational institutions of some sort.

The director's training ought to cover a broad, humanistic study with an artistic orientation. Literally everything a director can learn may prove useful in the theatre; he uses his total life experience as a resource for his work. His experience with other art forms can contribute richly. The director does well to study sculpture, painting, music, architecture, poetry, and literature, both to widen his aesthetic insights and to familiarize himself with different artistic techniques and intentions.

The Contemporary Situation for the Director

The director's relationship with the producer usually distinguishes the commercial theatre from the noncommercial theatre. In the commercial theatre, the producer, who organizes the production financially, first decides to stage a particular script. He then hires a director for that individual play. The director, the producer, and sometimes the playwright then select the cast and the remaining staff. The director may refuse the contract, of course, but the commercial director does not commonly enjoy great latitude in script selection. On the other hand, he usually deals with scripts from commercially successful playwrights and enjoys the excitement of staging world premieres. The Off- and Off-Off Broadway theatres seek commercial goals to a degree (some are non-profit operations funded by foundation grants), but tend more toward experimentation and avant-garde works. Similar companies operate comparably outside New York.

Regional professional companies, such as the Tyrone Guthrie in Minneapolis or the Loretto-Hilton in St. Louis, hire directors, actors, designers, and other staff members on a yearly basis for work in more than one production. Again, financial gain and artistic merit modify one another during the production schedule.

In the educational theatre, the director has more autonomy; the state government or the institutional administration "produces" the play. Production goals include both artistic merit and theatre education at the level appropriate to the public school, college, or university.

Community theatres often use their total membership as producers, and the organization may choose a director from the membership. Larger community theatres sometimes hire resident directors to supervise productions.

Directorial rewards include artistic merit and popular success, hopefully combined. The satisfaction of watching a successful and exciting opening night compares to that of coaching a successful athletic team or a similar cooperative effort. In commercial theatre, top salaries may exceed $5,000 a week.

College or university theatre directors receive an annual salary. Their responsibilities usually include teaching, administration, and research. Teaching loads often involve twelve or fifteen hours of student contact per week. A traditional approach credits the professor–director with three hours of released time from teaching for directing a major production. For the secondary-school teacher, theatre direction is usually an assumed part of the overall teaching position. Community-theatre directors, as stated earlier, may be hired by the year or may be volunteer members of the producing group.

Creative Procedures of the Director

As indicated earlier, how the script and the director come into contact depends in large part upon the nature of the producing agency: commercial, educational, or community. At some point, however, the director confronts a script that he plans to stage. Not all directors adhere to the following procedure; the approach typifies and describes the director's work in most cases.

Textual analysis prepares the director for his later work by giving him a profound understanding of the script. The director must first comprehend what the playwright intended when he wrote the script, whether or not he plans to follow those intentions. Methodology for script analysis varies immensely; and each director seeks his own way of studying a script. Some directors divide the script into "beats" or units of action, marking a division each time the stage action changes noticeably. Some scripts lend themselves to division by French scenes, that is, scenes marked by entrances or exits of characters. Structural analysis, based on determining the forces in conflict and following them toward eventual resolution, reveals a great deal about scripts dominated by the story element. Many directors favor Aristotelian analysis, based on the theories propounded in the *Poetics*. But use what method he will, the director first tries to peel away the script's verbiage, reveal the essential action, and discover the unique and individual form of the specific script.

At the same time, the director concerns himself with the practical matters of staging: cast size, costume requirements, lighting cues, setting demands, property needs, and so on. During early study, most directors prepare a production script or prompt script in which to record their responses at this stage of development. In this larger text of the script, the director has room for marginal notes and can insert materials relevant to his later work. A page from a typical prompt script is reproduced in Figure 3-2. Again, directorial techniques vary widely in this matter, as directors seek the means most efficient for them and for the specific script.

The distinction between words, which the playwright supplies, and actions, which underlie the dialogue, concerns the

Minestrone Macaroni,
Ravioli Aux Crevette,
Caramella In Padella,
Avocado Vinaigrette.

Scallopine Valdostana
Bisteccu Con Risotto,
Pasta Bolojnese
Pate Mayonnaise
Da Un Buon Appetito.

Minestrone Macaroni,
Ravioli Aux Crevette,
Caramella In Padella,
Avocado Vinaigrette.   †

†Singers continue verses
during next action.

[1]WAITRESS crosses to SR table and leaves tablecloth. WAITER 1 finishes setting chairs at DS table. HE starts to get broom[2], sees CARLO entering from SR and chases him into audience yelling in mock Italian. WAITRESS shakes out 3rd tablecloth[3], crosses to DS table as WAITER 1 crosses to USR table, passing her on bridge. HE fixes chairs and begins[4] sweeping SR area. WAITRESS places tablecloth on DS table. CARLO enters stage, sits at DS table in SR chair[5] and pinches her bottom. At first SHE doesn't react, then as HE persists SHE slaps him and begins to cross US. CARLO pulls tablecloth over him like a blanket and goes to sleep. WAITRESS sees him, screams at him in mock Italian, grabs[6] tablecloth, pulls him out of chair and throws him down SR stairs. HE yells at her in mock Italian and then begins talking to audience. WAIT-RESS fixes DS[7] tablecloth, crosses t~ USR table and with back to audience and fixes tablecloth.[8] CARLO sneaks up behind her, looks up her skirt, looks to audience and looks up her skirt again.[9] WAITRESS starts to cross to SL, CARLO climbs on mainstage and exits SR. WAITER 1 throws broom to HEADWAITER, goes down on knee and makes a pass at WAITRESS as SHE pushes him out of her way.   †

†Lyrics end – Melody of
"Minestrone Macaroni"
is hummed.

†Warn L. 3

[10]HEADWAITER throws his broom to WAITER 2 and makes a pass at WAITRESS as SHE pushes him out of the way. WAITER 2 throws both brooms to HEADWAITER[11] and falls on his knee and makes pass at WAITRESS. SHE slaps his face, crosses to SL table, straightens table-cloth,[12] and exits SL. [13]HEADWAITER throws both brooms to WAITER 1 and all[14] WAITERS cross to exit into café. HEADWAITER exits through café doors and bicycle horn is heard off SR. WAITERS 1

6b

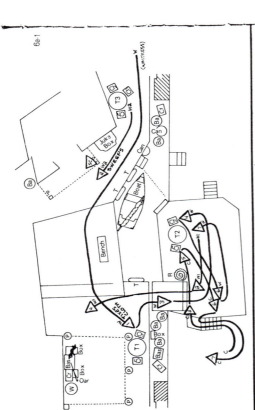

6a-1

6a-2

6a

director at this point. The theatre delineates life, and no more in a script than in real life does what a character says necessarily represent what he means or thinks. The great Russian director Stanislavski coined the term *subtext* to identify this aspect of analysis. This term is defined as "the thoughts or problems behind the dialogue." Stanislavski felt strongly that a script was not a finished piece of work until it was presented to an audience by actors, just as a musical score is not a symphony until played in concert by musicians. In both cases, Stanislavski maintained that the emotion of the performing artists brings the script or the score to life, releasing the inner essence of the work. When a play is performed, the words come from the author, the subtext from the actor. Without such a subtext, the words have no excuse for being presented to the public; they might just as well read the script at home. Directors and actors work together to discover the emotional circumstances of each scene with this subtext in mind.

Meetings with the other theatre artists properly follow the analytical stages of the director's work. Having come to a deep understanding of the script and a fully expressed production vision, the director prepares to articulate this vision to the designers and the producers. First, he may present them his overall vision of the production, then discuss with them the specific demands of that vision in terms of setting, lighting, costumes, makeup, and so on. Although the thoughtful director does not dictate specific methods to the designers, he shares his vision with them and insists that their contributions fit into the overall organic entity of the intended production. The designers' individuality modified by the total demands of the script as perceived by the direc-

FIGURE 3-2. *A page from the published prompt script of* Scapino *as produced by the Young Vic in London. The paths of the actors are indicated by heavy lines on the floor plan and are numbered to correspond to specific moments in the script. By permission of holder of rights to* Scapino, *the Dramatic Publishing Company, 4150 North Milwaukee Avenue, Chicago, Ill. 60641.*

tor requires the most delicate and sensitive communication and cooperation between all parties. In any case, the director makes the final decisions and approves all designs.

Traditionally the director next selects the actors to perform the roles. Some directors have suggested that casting determines 80 per cent of a show's success or failure, indicating the importance of the selection of the actors. In the commercial theatre, a performer of star rank may guarantee box office success, further complicating budgetary and aesthetic matters for the director; star status does not necessarily correspond with talent or appropriateness for a particular role. Nor does the director consider talent alone while choosing a cast. Each actor must correspond to the director's perception of the role, and each actor must mesh with the rest of the cast. Directors may sacrifice talent for appropriateness, especially in educational theatre. The director must cast the show as an organic whole, not merely as a succession of roles. Just as a football team could have too many quarterbacks and not enough linemen, a producing agency may have too many ingenues and not enough character men. Professional directors rarely face such problems; hundreds of performers may audition for a single role in the Broadway theatre, given the oversupply of talent and the scarcity of work for the professional actor. This oversupply can frequently result in "casting to type" or picking the actor physically closest to the role, rather than training a more talented actor to take on the characteristics of that role.

Overall most directors cast according to talent, experience, appropriateness to the specific role, and ability to relate to the rest of the cast. The educational theatre director may also consider the educational worth of the experience for the student actor; one may cast a less talented actor under these conditions.

With design elements under way and a cast selected, the director begins actual rehearsals. Again, creative procedures vary widely, but the overall pattern of activity moves from the general to the specific and back to the general, or from analysis through synthesis. A director deals with a script first as an entity, then dissects it into small bits, and then reassembles it according to his vision.

Many directors begin rehearsals by assembling the cast and having them read the play from beginning to end. During these rehearsals, the director can stop for discussions of the play's meaning and purpose and literally teach the cast the script. At this time, the director imparts and shares his goal for production with the cast. A full read-through gives the cast an overall concept of the script. At this point, the director urges the actors to consider the script as a whole and not yet to concern themselves with matters of interpretive detail. Properly, at this stage of rehearsal, they seek goals, not means. Actors and directors sometimes start acting and directing too soon, before they have made a clear determination of the potential dramatic actions and effects. In the early stages of rehearsal, the director is properly concerned with steeping the cast in the script and helping them to gain an intimate familiarity with that document, rather than striving for dramatic effect.

Directorial techniques in determining the placement and movement of actors upon the stage, usually called *blocking*, as opposed to gesture and posture, also vary widely from director to director and even for the same director staging different scripts. Some directors meticulously predetermine every movement prior to the first rehearsal, then dictate the movements to the cast. Such approaches seem appropriate for a highly stylized production, such as a Greek tragedy, a Restoration comedy, or comparable presentational theatre. Other directors block out only the entrances and exits and allow the actors to find their own patterns growing out of character motivations. This approach seems suitable for small-cast shows or scenes in which only a few actors appear. Many directors, however, prefer to preplan the physical arrangements to avoid wasting rehearsal time in experimentation.

69

Any competent director will remain open to changing any preplanned arrangement if rehearsal reveals a preferable alternative. Some blocking patterns, seemingly effective on paper, fail when attempted with actual actors. All concerned must then seek alternatives. Ideally all blocking supports and amplifies the play's action, giving the audience yet another set of visual stimuli leading to a fuller appreciation of the actions portrayed. The director seeks, especially on a proscenium stage, to stage the most important events in the strongest possible position for audience reception. In arena or thrust staging, the director faces different problems in making the action visible. With the audience surrounding the acting area from 250° to 360° in full round, the visual presentation of the actors must constantly change to ensure sufficient visibility.

The bulk of the rehearsal period follows blocking rehearsals. These rehearsals seek to flesh out characterization, determine techniques and business, set details, determine and regulate the most appropriate pace, define actions and motivations, and deal with the myriad details of staging. During this period, director and actors continue to probe beyond the written text to find the underlying motivations, actions, and goals. In short, they determine the actions in which the words are imbedded. The division of the script into beats, or units of action, properly leads the cast away from mere vocalism and into the proper work of the actor, action. No detail is too small for consideration during these rehearsals, but the director seeks to use the time most efficiently to cover all the matters of concern. The cast and the director can get lost in details; the cast should have an occasional uninterrupted runthrough of a scene, act, or the entire script in order to refresh their concept of the total script. Bit by bit, they dissect and analyze the script, then reassemble it into an organic entity to be presented as the play.

Eight or ten rehearsals prior to opening, most directors use runthroughs exclusively, allowing the actors to rehearse the entire play, while the director takes notes and discusses any problems with the cast either between acts or after the rehearsal. After a few such runthroughs, technical elements are introduced: lighting, sound, costumes, makeup, the completed setting, and properties. Some directors prefer to spend one long rehearsal adding all these elements; others prefer to let them gradually come into the rehearsals, some light cues one night, some another, the more difficult costumes early, others later, and so on. During the week prior to opening, however, the final assembly of the play takes place, and the last few rehearsals seek to approximate performance situations as closely as possible. Some directors invite audiences to the last rehearsals, enabling their actors to begin the interaction with an audience. In any case, the cast should face as few changes as possible, ideally none, on the opening night; the audience's presence will provide sufficient challenge.

After the show opens, the cast continues its work to perfect its execution. During a run, in repertory, the director can often hold additional rehearsals of either troublesome scenes or the entire show. In the commercial theatre, the stage manager takes charge of the production and may call additional rehearsals at his discretion, and the director may in some cases return. In the educational theatre, schedules do not often permit such additional rehearsals, although more and more university, college, and high-school directors continue polishing a production through the final performance.

Audience response ususally dictates such changes during a show's run. During the rehearsal period, all the theatre artists—director, playwright, actors, designers, and technicians—have use used their expertise, creativity, and experience to predict audience response. No prediction can be entirely accurate, given the variations in audiences and artists, so just as a football defense changes to meet a particular offense, so does a producing company alter its techniques to achieve greater communion with its patrons.

FIGURE 3-3A. *While an assistant director follows the script, the director and another assistant director evaluate the scene in progress. Permission from Southern Illinois University—Edwardsville.*

FIGURE 3-3B. *The director discusses various options with the cast, hoping to improve the scene. Permission from Southern Illinois University—Edwardsville.*

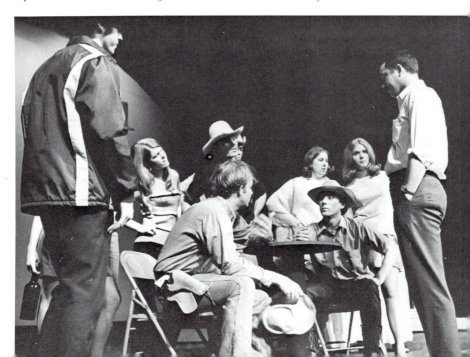

FIGURE 3-3C. *The cast rehearses the scene again. Permission from Southern Illinois University—Edwardsville.*

FIGURE 3-3D. *After the addition of costumes, properties, and makeup, the cast performs the scene as rehearsed. Permission from Southern Illinois University—Edwardsville.*

Evaluating the Director's Contribution

In the theatre, a performing art that cannot truly exist until presented to an audience, audience reception seems the first and only criterion of judgment. The director, who is responsible for the entire production, would appear especially liable to such judgment.

As in the case of the playwright, audience–critics may well have great difficulty distinguishing the director's contributions from those of the other theatre artists. For example, the efforts and results merge and distinctions blur between the actor's art and the director's guidance. A director may stage a superb script and fail to achieve its potential; inexperienced directors rarely do Shakespeare well, for example. On the other hand, a director may take a mediocre script and give it a brilliant performance, or an exceptional cast may bring a script to a life far beyond that envisioned by the playwright.

But if in the modern theatre the director selects the script, casts and rehearses the actors, and approves all artistic elements of the production, he must bear primary responsibility for the overall production.

Once again, audience–critics may use the three Goethe questions suggested in Chapter Three: What was the artist trying to do? How well did he do it? Was it worth doing? The director's contribution to a production seems even less tangible than the playwright's, hence the desirability of some systematic approach to evaluation.

An audience may make no effort to perceive the director's intentions, reducing the possibility of a successful transaction. If the director does not consider his audience's experience and degree of theatrical sophistication, the odds for success decrease. A successful theatrical experience requires mutual respect and effort on both sides of the proscenium arch; the audience must remain open to new aesthetic possibilities and must not enter the theatre with preconceived concepts, and the director must not indulge himself in his own artistic pursuits without considering the nature of his audience.

Two dangers exist here. One is that the audience will consider the theatre artists as mere Bohemians, a group of self-centered exhibitionists fondling one another on stage with no concern for the audience. The other is that the theatre artists may come to consider the audience as Philistines, sensation-seeking dullards incapable of artistic enjoyment. Such hostile circumstances doom the possibility of a successful artistic interaction.

Goethe's second question—How well did the artist succeed in achieving his intentions—asks the audience-member to judge the work by his previous experience and knowledge. Because theatre properly seeks an effect of some sort on the audience, if the audience-critic can determine that sought-for effect, he can speak with some certainty as to whether or not the production achieved that effect upon him, personally. Whether or not the production affected the rest of the audience in the same way is more difficult to determine. Because audiences vary considerably and audience responses vary widely from one performance to another, overall judgment of a play's success or failure would ideally require having seen an entire run or at least a representative sampling of all productions. The concept of a play's being re-created in every performance thus becomes a matter of great practicality in evaluation. Tastes and expectations vary from individual to individual; audiences are groups of individuals. Any audience member is perfectly justified in saying that he does or does not like a particular artwork or production, but he needs wider evidence and credentials for suggesting that the work was good or bad. Because no final arbiters of aesthetic truth exist, critics or analysts have the opportunity of illuminating theatrical experiences, offering a broader base for our personal judgments.

75

Goethe's third question—whether or not what the artist sought to do was worth doing in the first place—an audience answers subjectively as their life experiences collide with those expressed by the total producing agency. They may or may not agree; an audience seeking superficial entertainment of the popular variety will find Brecht, Shaw, or Greek tragedy a terrible bore. The audience member seeking beautiful language and poetry, philosophical ideas, and delineations of the modern man's existential dilemma will not find them in *Hello, Dolly!* Fortunately most of us have broad bases for appreciation. Most people sometimes want only entertainment and diversion and other times seek the challenge of more substantial aesthetic experience; lack of variety fosters monotony. Given the pressures of modern life, the diversionary aspects of most modern theatre appeal to a wider audience than does serious drama, and most past periods reveal comparable situations. Even the didactic German playwright Bertolt Brecht pointed out that theatre ought to be above all entertaining; other functions follow.

Perhaps the modern idioms of "Different strokes for different folks" and "Whatever turns you on" relate to this problem. Certainly judgment of the director's work reveals the interdependency of theatrical audiences and artists, a relationship sometimes overlooked but always present and foremost in theatrical excellence. No one has yet written a definitive history of theatre audiences, but theatre history reveals a few eras when artist and audience were of a single mind, both nurturing the other, both stimulating the other to heights neither could achieve alone. In the modern theatre, audience and artists sometimes achieve a oneness constituting an impressive experience for both. The director leads the quest for such experiences.

Although the audience rarely has direct awareness of it, the director's relationship with the other theatre artists affects the production considerably. A harmonious working situation usually produces better art, and the director assumes responsibility for the creative atmosphere. Directors who vent their aesthetic frustration by fits of rage and shouting rarely produce anything except jangled nerves and hostility, and the eventual production as viewed by the audience loses much of its full potential. Groups of people working toward a common goal need calm leadership in the modern theatre.

Conclusions

The future theatre will continue to call for talented and innovative directors. The need for excellence will not diminish. Children's theatre grows in significance and worth; community theatre begins to regain some of the luster it had during the 1920s and 1930s; educational theatre continues to increase the quality of production; and the commercial theatre seems always to find its audience when the productions have merit. Many of the old traditions of staging and directing fade into disuse; new rehearsal techniques constantly emerge; multimedia productions call for skills unknown to previous directors. Above all, the director's work with the actor in rehearsal continues to demand qualities rare in any profession.

Chapter Four

The Actor

"An actor is a man standing on a stage in a three hundred dollar suit with holes in his underwear."
—*Old Vaudeville Joke*

JOHN F. KENNEDY had a favorite poem:

Bullfight critics ranked in rows
Crowd the enormous Plaza full;
But only one is there who knows—
And he's the man who fights the bull.
—DOMINGO ORTEGA, *translated by Robert Graves.*

All the contributions of other theatre artists notwithstanding, the actor alone "fights the bull." The actor's work literally constitutes the play in production. He has the most direct and immediate interaction with the audience, and he alone can respond to audience reaction during actual performance. The actor is the primary medium, the essential means by which a production reaches the audience. Perhaps the public's traditional fascination with performers stems from the directness of their relationship during production. Actors literally work with and for the audience, the per-

79

FIGURE 4-1. *The actor exercises his personal creativity each time he faces a new audience. Permission from Southern Illinois University—Edwardsville.*

former's function being to stimulate an appropriate response to an appropriate degree from each audience.

The actor's contributions to a production closely and substantially relate to those by the other theatre artists. An actor rarely improves a performance; playwrights predetermine his words, and stage directions dictate most of his actions. The designers create the scenic and costume environments in which the actor works, thereby limiting the performer's choices of movement. The theatre architects have impact upon the actor's work as well (consider seating capacity and its effect upon vocal projection and size of gesture), although the actor usually arrives at the theatre long after the architect has finished his work.

The actor usually interacts most directly with the director. The director needs from the actor the living presence that makes up actual production; the actors look to the director for objective evaluation of their work, for guidance, and for leadership during rehearsal and performance. Without the actors, the director has nothing to direct; without the director, the actors could perform but would as a cast risk losing the cohesiveness and unity required for excellence. As so often happened in past ages before the advent of the director, the cast might wander along as a collection of individual performers, lacking central purpose or goal; they would then create by committee.

The Actor's Alternatives and Restrictions

No artist encounters more obvious or evident limitations of self than the actor. Most artists work with some material or instrument—the painter with paint and canvas, the musician with his instrument, and so on—but the actor operates simultaneously as both artist and instrument, both creator and the thing created. The playwright puts limits on the ac-

81

tor's characterization, to be sure, as does the director, but during production and much of rehearsal, the actor pursues his art alone in a crowd.

Physical limitations restrict the actor; he cannot play all roles (at least not sensibly) because of his physical qualities; John Wayne will probably never play Juliet, and he would make an unlikely Romeo. Age, sex, coloring, weight, height, race, and vocal characteristics weigh heavily as obviously considered attributes when a director casts an actor. Even mimes often suffer frustration because they cannot turn themselves into any person, animal, or object desired. As one mime recently put it, "The bones keep getting in the way." The modern actor finds himself comparably limited.

Directors considering an actor for a role must consider both vocal characteristics and vocal ability. An audience properly demands to hear and understand an actor, and whereas the film or television actor has the advantage of electronic amplification, the stage actor faces the problems of projection and articulation in each performance; vocal stamina becomes a major consideration. So too does the actor's vocal quality or uniqueness. Vocal quality depends upon the physical characteristics of the vocal mechanism and the speaker's vocal techniques: Laurence Olivier, Walter Brennan, and Anthony Quinn present remarkably different vocal personalities.

The actor's psychic limitations, his intellectual and emotional ranges, constitute a more abstract concept but an extremely concrete problem. Although the physical and vocal aspects of acting make up the essential craft of the art, the actor's use of his spiritual resources can lead him to genius or doom him to mediocrity. As in any art, acting emanates from the artist's total psyche. His past experiences, his vision of life, his aesthetic philosophy, his relationship with other artists and audiences, in short, the total makeup of his personality comes into essential play when he is approaching or performing a role. Similarly politicians speak of a candidate's being "big enough" for a governorship but not for a presidency; athletes speak of heart; singers mention soul when describing another singer. Some critics analyze an artwork's aesthetic size; *Macbeth* is considered a "bigger" script than *As You Like It;* Michelangelo's "Pieta" does not encompass so much as his "David." Not every actor has the internal resources for Hamlet, Lady Macbeth, or Oedipus.

Detection and expansion of these psychic limits properly concern actors, acting teachers, and directors. Although actors have struggled with this matter from the very beginning, the work of Konstantin Stanislavski, the great Russian director at the turn of this century, typifies modern acting theory, and his contributions to the training of the contemporary actor have had major significance. The interested student will find further material listed in the Bibliography.

As previously noted, the visions of the playwright and the director set certain boundaries upon an actor's work. The playwright's given circumstances for the character, the character's dialogue, and the director's interpretation of both are major factors in the actor's approach to his role. Just as some canvases are larger for a painter, so are some roles for an actor, but the actor seeks freedom within his limitations. Actors who refuse to play small roles have little value for a producing agency. Such "actors" usually equate acting solely with exhibitionism. Financial concerns complicate the commercial theatre, of course, but the old theatrical adage, "There are no small roles, only small actors," still rings true.

The audience limits or modifies the actor's work. Acting at its highest levels seeks to stimulate a oneness of spirit and emotion between performers and audience, and some audiences are more receptive to such stimulation than others. Such oneness entails extremely complex matters, such as the socioeconomic background of the audience, their theatrical experience, the actor's reputation, all other elements of the production, and much more. The specific nature of each audience modifies each performance to a greater or lesser degree, however. In a very real sense, the audience defines theatrical quality on their terms.

83

Those terms may or may not be supported by future developments. Although audience rejection rarely indicates that a bright new actor is emerging, most of the world's great actors met massive rejection at some time in their careers, usually in the early stages. English audiences hissed Sir Henry Irving—perhaps the world's leading actor at the turn of this century—off the stage in his first appearance. A critic described Laurence Olivier as resembling a belligerent sparrow when he first played Romeo in New York. When the great English actor Edmund Kean made his first appearance as Hamlet, a critic at the time called him "one of the vilest figures that has been seen either on or off the stage. . . . As for his Hamlet, it is one of the most terrible misrepresentations to which Shakespeare has ever been subjected." A few years later, Kean had completely conquered the London theatre; the English-speaking world considered him the world's greatest actor. For a time, a public accustomed to one set of theatrical traditions may react with confusion or hostility to new theatrical methods, and innovation in any human endeavor may war with the inertia of tradition. Departures from the norm will quite literally encounter the test of time. Hopefully a temporal art appeals to the audience at the time of its creation.

If the actor faces such limitations, so too does he encounter unique rewards and satisfactions as a performer. The stage actor receives immediate response to his work; onlookers evaluate his work immediately and unmistakably. Furthermore, if his work does not go well, he will soon have another chance to modify, correct, or improve it in another performance. This opportunity is double-edged; should the actor achieve a brilliant moment of rapport with the audience, he faces a new audience for the next performance, and he must find a way to repeat that moment. Some inexperienced actors err by "trying to play last night's show"; few, if any, succeed. Even the actor who many consider today to be the greatest living performer, Laurence Olivier, encountered this frustration during his brilliantly successful run of *Othello* at the National Theatre in London in 1965, if a widely circulated anecdote is to be believed. Fellow actors report that one evening Olivier achieved an outstanding success with the Moor, one of those evening when new heights were achieved, leaving audience and cast alike stunned. After the audience's ovations, Olivier stormed into his dressing room, slammed the door, and raged furiously about, quite to the dismay of his startled fellow players. Finally one of them mustered sufficient courage to suggest to Olivier that he had no idea why the great star was so disturbed; it seemed that the evening had gone brilliantly. Olivier snarled a reply, "Yes, it *was* brilliant, but I don't know if I can ever do it again!"

Above all the actor's art is intensely personal. The actor mounts the public platform and actually executes the show. That satisfaction remains his and his alone. The successful actor literally leads and shapes the imagination of an audience. The fulfillment of such an endeavor offers much more than merely ego satisfaction; it offers the pleasure of having succeeded in a shared experience.

More practical rewards await the actor. Salaries for a few top professionals may run to $5,000 a week for stage actors or $1 million per film. Obviously the vast majority of actors receive nowhere near these figures, but the prospect of incredible affluence always beckons. Actors also seek the respect of their fellow workers, always a professional and social concern. For actors in all types of theatre, the social aspects of their group efforts contribute to a sense of belonging, just as for others in our society membership in a fraternal group, a religious group, a hobby group, or the like affiliates the member with something larger than himself. People who share an intense interest in a common activity seem to present a closed perimeter to outsiders. Their togetherness grows from shared experiences and interests.

In college and university theatre, the educational aspects of theatre production can offer the actor remarkable gains. Everyone seeks new experiences. The actor seeks out not only his own experience but, in dealing with a character-ization, those of a created personality. Properly approached by actor, director, and teacher, the study and exercise of acting amplifies a person's self-awareness and adds to his insight into others' human characteristics. Education at all levels seeks precisely the same goals.

Requisites of Excellence in Acting

The concept of talent, a word bandied about in most of the arts and sciences, leads to endless confusion; literally every-one talks about it and no one quite defines it. In the theatre, however, talent for an actor seems related to the ability to create a reality on a stage, a reality growing out of the cir-cumstances of the character and the situation depicted in the script. This ability may at first seem hypocritical or re-lated to living a falsehood, and this aspect of the theatre has disturbed moralists from the beginning. Again the critic must separate techniques and goals; the actor creates his re-ality within a characterization for an aesthetic rather than a opportunistic end. A child pretends to be a superhero for his own pleasure, not for subterfuge; acting has about the same relationship to childhood games as childish drawing and scribbling does to painting or literature. The actor must not believe that he literally is the character, lest he risk schizophrenia, but he, like the audience, must willingly and temporarily suspend disbelief and accept illusion for aes-thetic goals. This ability to control one's imagination for the creation of an illusion marks the beginning of acting talent.

This ability will not suffice if the actor lacks an expressive, flexible voice and body with which to embody his creation. Again, a pianist may have superb skills, but if he has an in-adequate piano, he cannot succeed. The actor must control body, mind, and voice to present repetitively what he has created in rehearsals.

86

The nonactor scarcely imagines the stamina needed for such work. The old truism "Art conceals art," applies to most theatre endeavors; what appears easy, natural, and graceful in production usually results from rigorous effort in rehearsal. Substantial work in the theatre demands much of the performer, both physically and psychically. If the actor has a long role, he must sustain it throughout long rehearsals or performances; with a short role, he must keep himself ready during long and enervating periods of waiting to expend his energy at the proper moment. In either case, performers soon realize that acting well demands physical conditioning and mental stamina.

An interesting parallel exists between the actor's work during rehearsal and that of the jazz musician or the athlete during practice. A football player, for example, does not actually play football during practices. Even in intrasquad scrimmages in which a score is kept, the game is not a real one. Rather the athlete seeks to sharpen his skills as a player in conditions as close as possible to an actual game. Football is played only between two opposing teams, and until the other team arrives, no game is possible, only preparation. Similarly jazz, being based on musical improvisation, can be prepared for, but it cannot be actually executed except at the moment of creation. Jam sessions, so popular with jazz players, are merely sessions in which the musicians play for one another, but without an audience of some sort, the musician is in the same preparatory stage as the actor rehearsing to an empty auditorium.

Other factors contribute to excellence. Physical appeal, charisma, and attractiveness, frequently overrated, nevertheless have marketable potential. They can have value to the actor, especially in productions stressing the actor's personality or charm rather than his artistry. Although such productions are somewhat more decorative than substantial, they have supplied entertainment and diversion to millions and hold a definite place in the theatrical spectrum. Unhappily, when such a performer's appeal fades, as fade it must, so does his career, as exemplified by hundreds of child stars or sex symbols who could not deal with their own maturity.

Professionals frequently mention luck as a major factor in their careers, often putting the ratio at 90 per cent luck to 10 per cent talent. To be sure, sheer chance will affect any profession so oversupplied with talent. The young commercial actor, making the seemingly endless rounds of agencies in New York or Los Angeles, must realize that he constitutes simultaneously not only artist and instrument but in a larger sense a one-man small-business operation. He is simultaneously the product, the public-relations man, the packager, and the package. As all people must to a certain degree, the actor must "sell" himself to an available market. Perhaps such a commercial circumstance alienates many young artistic idealists, but the young actor needs pragmatism. Before he plays Hamlet, he may well play bit parts or deodorant commercials. His creativity may burn with a hard and gemlike flame, but he also has to make a living.

The training of the actor is obviously complex and never-ending, and nowhere in the United States at this time may the apprentice actor enroll in a long-term, comprehensive training program. Most actors received their earliest training and experiences in educational institutions, gaining further training either in conservatory situations or by actual professional work. These types of training have value. Both have contributed many excellent actors to American theatre, but neither prepares performers as efficiently as might be desired. The educational situation often protects the student actor from the hard, cold facts of getting a job or the competition in the commercial theatre. Conservatory programs, with their usual commercial orientation, too often neglect the education of the total person while concentrating upon theatrical skills. Perhaps from experiencing both types of training the student can gain a total overview, but often the student must put things together himself on his own. Several institutions have recently sought to alleviate these unfortunate circumstances.

In any event, the actor's training should begin with the preparation of the instrument, the actor's body and voice. This training must continue for the actor's entire career and should constitute a daily regimen for any performer. Also, psychological training in concentration, sensory awareness, interpersonal relationships, sensitivity, and similar techniques should begin early in the actor's training. He must likewise pursue this study as long as he considers acting his vocation.

An actor's background in aesthetics and other arts can contribute to the taste with which he shapes his performance, and can give him a sense of proportion about his work. The actor should especially read widely in dramatic literature and the heritage of his art.

Perhaps most important, the actor's training ought to lead him to a lifelong study of nature, that is, the life from which he draws his art. What seems to the onlooker like egocentricity and self-centeredness in performing artists may be the artist's study of himself in varying situations. Many excellent actors have, when overwhelmed by private, personal griefs, made mental notes on their reactions in order to use them later on stage. If everyman is truly in every man, if each of us contains in microcosm the totality of human qualities, such seemingly callous self-observation can often prove invaluable to the actor. At the same time, the actor must carefully study the varieties of human action and reaction from the heights to the depths in order to have at his command both an understanding of and a sympathy for the spectrum of characters he may attempt.

Actors must find a spark of sympathy, indeed love, for each role they play. They must find, even for the most hideous and despicable of characters, the understandable motivation that generates the action of that character within his circumstances. Sir Laurence Olivier described what he considers the best advice anyone ever gave him. In 1944 he played Sergius in Bernard Shaw's *Arms and the Man* at the Old Vic in London. As he put it:

Well, that night Tony Guthrie came to see the performance, and . . . from his great height, looked down at me and said, "Liked your Sergius very much." And I snarled and said, "Oh, thank you very much, too kind, I'm sure." And he said, "No, no. Why, what's the matter?" And I said, "Well, really, don't ask . . . no, please." And he said, "But don't you love Sergius?" And I said, "Look, if you weren't so tall, I'd hit you. How do you mean, how can you love a part like that, a stupid, idiot part? Absolutely nothing to do but conform, to provide the cues for Shaw's ideas of what was funny at the time. How can you possibly enjoy or like a part like that?" And he said, "Well, of course, if you can't love Sergius, you'll never be any good in him, will you?" Well, it clicked, and something happened, I suppose, that gave me a new attitude, perhaps an attitude that had been completely lacking in me, up to that time, towards the entire work of acting. (Laurence Olivier–Kenneth Tynan interview, BBC television, 1967).

Actors must experience life before they can illuminate it, so the individual actor must experience—if not always widely, then certainly deeply—to enrich his supply of creative resources.

The Contemporary Situation for the Actor

Actors Equity is the stage actors' professional union in this country. Horror stories emanate from New York City regularly about how low a percentage of Equity actors earn a living at their profession. Most commercial actors require some other skill or profession to enable them to live from day to day while they seek employment. The unhappy circumstances may explain to audiences some of the desperation involved in the profession and the difficulty in obtaining work or the delight an actor may express when hired for a television commercial. Several hundred performers may answer an audition call for a single role, and the preliminary "interviews" begin with only a few seconds' examination of each applicant to eliminate the majority. *A Chorus Line* dramatizes these circumstances as applied to Broadway dancers by presenting in musical comedy form the selection of eight dancers out of nearly thirty finalists. We are all constantly being evaluated by others for various reasons and by various standards. The rejection of the majority of the dancers in *A Chorus Line* evoked sympathy in most of its audiences, winning it substantial success on Broadway.

Faced with such competition, many young performers grow discouraged and leave the profession. Because the theatre has such lure, however, and promises such fame and fortune, many thousands stay, even though only a small minority will rise, through talent, persistence, love of their art, and sheer luck, to the top.

In the regional theatres, the actor may find greater security and artistic satisfaction. The professional repertory companies outside New York City usually offer contracts on an annual basis, renewable if justified by the demands of the company and the actor's work. Actors in such situations do not often receive national exposure. New York still represents the hub of American theatre and the mecca for stage actors. Larger audiences and larger potential income from financial investment still center on the East Coast, although the rise of regional theatres suggests a decentralization process. Whether the professional theatre will eventually permeate the entire nation, as many theater artists hope, remains speculation.

The increasing affiliations between professional and educational theatre groups offers some hope for the future. Universities offer greater security, professional groups often bring greater experience and expertise, and such alliances may combine the best of both. The key to such ventures lies in articulation and acceptance of common goals

91

between two groups with sharply contrasting traditions. If either allies only for purposes of self-serving prestige, the potential for excellence withers.

Students actors rarely receive payment from universities. Their work constitutes a means to an end, not the end itself. Student actors act to increase their theatrical understanding through practical experience. Although they may attain high proficiency, they can rarely attain the expertise of a performer who has spent a lifetime perfecting his art and practicing his craft. Athletics offer an obvious parallel: college football, although rarely as well executed, frequently generates more excitement than professional football. Usually the amateur brings commitment and enthusiasm; the professional offers expertise and experience.

Community theatre actors are usually avocational performers, though again they may achieve a high quality. Some, indeed, bring considerable professional or university experience to their work, and the festivals of the American Community Theatre Association often present excellent theatre. The Little Theatre movement of early twenth-century America, essentially a community theatre operation, achieved a dramatic renaissance, giving opportunity to several major playwrights then in the early stages of development.

Creative Procedures for the Actor

The actor's work divides into two categories: first, the general work of self-improvement to increase his potential as an artist, and second, the specific work in preparing a role for production.

In the final analysis, the first type of work includes all the actor's life experiences. More obvious techniques would include daily vocal drills, often under the tutelage of a vocal coach. Actors in the modern theatre often audition for sing-

92

ing roles, adding another dimension to vocal study; one's singing voice, like one's speaking voice, never attains perfection.

Successful actors frequently work out regularly in gymnasiums, just as athletes do, and for much the same reasons. While muscular development may or may not be desirable for the performer, muscle tone and stamina are almost always demanded of him. Dance classes, as well as increasing an obviously marketable skill, also serve the purpose of physical conditioning.

The actor does well to steep himself in the theatre, of course, by attending the theatre whenever possible and by reading widely in all aspects of his art. Incredibly many young actors read only those scripts for which they intend to audition, whereas experienced and successful performers tend to follow theatrical developments with some care.

Development of one's aesthetic sensibility often occupies the successful artist of any kind. Actors profit from exposure to excellence of any sort, but especially in the other fine arts. The mind-expanding experience of modern art may well stimulate a sharpened sense of innovation in the modern actor.

Finally, the actor can and should pursue his craft by the continued study of acting itself. In New York, for example, several studios hold classes not just for beginners but for successful and working professionals. Lee Strasberg, for instance, helped found the Actors Studio for just such a purpose, and the HB Studio has a similar purpose and is equally admired. A relatively complete list of such non-collegiate schools is found in *Simon's Directory of Theatrical Materials, Services, and Information.*

To facilitate this sort of personal and artistic growth, modern acting teachers have devised a vast number of techniques, including improvisations and theatrical games. These serve as either warm-up exercises for rehearsal or performance or a general technique to free the actor from inhibition and blocks to his creativity.

The reader may well have heard the song "Nothing" from the musical comedy *A Chorus Line,* in which a young actress named Morales is browbeaten by a fraudulent acting teacher for failing to "feel the motion" of an imaginary bobsled. (Morales suspects that her failure may be genetic; she didn't have bobsleds in San Juan.) Such techniques can nevertheless be immensely useful to the actor, but only if led by a teacher with imagination and concern for the individual; charlatans appear in every profession. And improvisational work has much to offer only if the actor is clear in his own mind about why he is participating in such work. Improvisation is a means, not an end.

Although a somewhat advanced technique, recalling physical sensations can assist the actor considerably in creating an internal and honest emotion on a stage. More obviously, if an actor swathed in furs with a stage temperature of more than 90° seeks to present an illusion of bitter cold, as in the opening scene of *Hamlet,* the value of Morales's imaginary bobsled may emerge as fairly practical.

Those who are not theater artists (and many who are) often find such mental gymnastics highly amusing; an actor straining to represent a tree, a piece of frying bacon, or a sports car has some aspects of the ludicrous if not the grotesque. But such exercises can free the actor physically and mentally. A performer may be able to approach a character more efficiently for having played a cigar butt; indeed, he may find a certain area of commonality between a cigar butt—wet, soggy, brown, raveled, gross, and nasty—and some characters. Farfetched? Perhaps, but if an artist thinks something helps, it does.

So too with exercise games such as the very popular "Mirrors." In "Mirrors," actors pair off, face to face. One initiates actions, usually very slowly at first; the other tries to reflect those actions as closely as possible. Ideally an onlooker cannot tell which player initiates and which reflects. Although such activity may well startle the local custodial force, it does help an actor achieve nonverbal communication with another person, an obligatory skill for successful acting. The exercise of concentration in this game develops that capacity in the performer. If students try this exercise seriously, they will find other benefits as well.

Actors and acting teachers steadily continue to seek new techniques for training. Many are soon discarded, but others win approval by bringing substantial gains to artistic development.

The second aspect of the actor's work, that of preparing a specific role, although varying widely from performer to performer, usually follows a three-part pattern. First, the actor analyzes the script and his role in it to determine appropriate goals. Second, he finds the means to achieve those goals. And third, he seeks means of retaining those achievements during the run of the performance.

Analysis for the actor parallels that of the director, but with a narrower focus on one role. The actor must study the entire script and relate his portion of it, no matter how small, to the overall production intention. Again, procedures vary, but actors often begin by carefully reading and rereading the script to discover the given circumstances of the role: where and when it takes place, what information about the character is specifically delineated by the playwright, his relations with the other characters, his goals, what complicates his achievement of those goals, and so on. Playwrights rarely supply all of the necessary details, so the actor and the director must create them. A few such character aspects include parentage, education, religious background, sexual preferences and experiences, physical qualities, economic status, and so on. Literally an actor seeks to determine these circumstances as far back as the character's grandparents and tries to create a character history leading up to the script's first events. Some actors find speculation about the character's actions after the script ends helpful. For example, what will happen to and what will be done by, Horatio after the Danish court has been cleared of the bodies of Hamlet, Claudius, Laertes, and Gertrude? How will

Horatio fare under the reign of Fortinbras? Although this sort of speculation may seem inconsequential, any such investigative speculation can lead to a more three-dimensional characterization and hence increase audience appreciation.

At the same time, many actors try to discover in the character some aspects of themselves, those facets of the character speaking most vividly to the actor or some point of connection between the actor and the character. No definitive characterization can exist. Because of the very nature of theatre and acting, the actor's personality will modify the enacted role. Thus Hamlets played by Laurence Olivier, Richard Burton, and Richard Chamberlain differ, partly because of the different intentions of the actors and the directors and partly because of the different qualities and personalities of the performers. No idealized characterization of any role exists, only the most effective a particular actor can attain.

Many actors can find within their own personalities qualities useful in preparing and playing a role. Playing "villains" illustrates this process clearly. No character truly thinks of himself as a villain; villainy as a concept represents social evaluation from an external point of view. A Richard III, an Adolph Hitler, a torturer of the Spanish Inquisition, a hired murderer, each has in some way justified his actions to himself. Although he may realize clearly that his actions vary from the laws or mores of society, he has elected to follow a "villainous" course of action for some reason or in response to some act perpetrated on him. He has justified himself. The actor's responsibility includes finding the germ of truth in that justification, a germ that he can himself recognize, even though he may not condone it. This willing suspension of moral disbelief calls for a wide and sympathetic understanding of human action. Guthrie's advice to Olivier referred not only to the shallow and stupid Sergius but to all roles.

Actors use different "points of attack" in preparing a role for the stage. Some may work internally, seeking a psycho-

96

logical basis for the role. In the United States, such an approach is commonly associated with the Actors Studio and Lee Strasberg; such actors as Marlon Brando, Ben Gazzara, Rod Steiger, Eli Wallach, and Joanne Woodward received training in this tradition.

Other actors prefer an external approach, beginning with some physical aspect of characterization as a basis for development. Laurence Olivier, for example, has suggested that he constructs his characterizations from the outside with the role traveling inward later. Other actors such as Hume Cronyn profess similar approaches.

Debate has raged for centuries about the role of emotion in the actor's work, with no sign of resolution in sight. Actors clearly need a highly developed external technique for the stage, just as they must remain open to internal emotional response during rehearsal and performance. In so intensely personal an art as acting, each artist seeks his own method to combine his own individuality with the demands of the role. Perhaps Joseph Jefferson III (1829–1905), a highly successful American actor, came closest to putting the problem in proper perspective when he advocated "a warm heart and a cool head" as the ideal wedding of intellect and emotion.

The second stage of role preparation seeks the most effective methods of expressing the script's action to the audience. Here the actor depends more upon the director, who watches the actor's attempts, his trials and errors, and seeks to guide him toward his highest potential. Although an actor may evaluate himself and his work while acting, he finds this approach difficult and error-prone at best. Such judgment accumulates only after decades of experience, and even then the actor must seek corroboration from someone he trusts; ideally, the director.

At this point in rehearsal, the actor determines many of the variables of dialogue vocalization and the infinite variety of movement and gesture. The actor does not work as a mere robot, but he seeks a pattern of action for his role. Although no absolute rules exist in art, certain traditions about stage acting persist because they frequently represent the most effective method for some piece of stage business. For example, an actor usually moves more gracefully across the stage if he starts with his upstage foot, the one furthest from the audience. Similar, most actors habitually reach with an upstage hand, employ curved rather than straight moves, enter a door or sit in a chair in a certain way, when appropriate to the circumstances. Audiences don't usually notice these traditions, but they beget a smoothness contributing to the audience's appreciation.

The third step of role preparation involves keeping the performance fresh and seemingly spontaneous. During rehearsals, stage action fluctuates markedly. During the first week or so of performance, the cast responds to audience reactions and can easily concentrate on the relative novelty of the performance. But after a few weeks, a few months, in some cases a few years, performances can grow stale and tired, and the actor must find ways to keep a sense of vitality and life in his performance. An American actor, William Gillette (1855–1937), coined the phrase "the illusion of the first time" for this aspect of acting. An actor repeats his role hundreds of times through rehearsal and performance, and he faces the danger of "walking through his role," that is, mere mechanical repetition. Because only one substantial element, the audience, varies from performance to performance, most actors eagerly seize upon the variations in audience responses and use them to make each performance a new event. Others combine this approach with small variations of their performances, or they keep studying their role, trying to find fresh insights and nuances in their character. Mrs. Sarah Siddons (1755–1831), an outstanding English actress, played Lady Macbeth intermittently for thirty years, yet she spent the morning before each performance studying the part and reading the entire script. She almost always found something new in it, "something which had not struck me as much as it *ought* to have struck me," as she

98

FIGURE 4-2A. *William Gillette (1855–1937), an American actor who advanced a more natural style of acting during his career.*

put it. Continued exploration of this sort, the eternal quest for the perfect performance enables the actor not only to survive but to grow in his art during long runs.

In summary, the actor seeks his goals and identifies them, then determines the means by which he might reasonably expect to achieve those goals in performance, and finally determines how to continue to sustain them through a series of performances. Great individual variation exists, but actors of all times and places have faced comparable problems in creating their roles.

FIGURE 4-2B. *Mrs. Sarah Siddons (1755–1831), one of the great English actresses of all time. From the author's personal collection.*

Evaluating the Actor's Contribution

The actor's work combines so intimately with that of the playwright and the director that making precise evaluations is a difficult matter. The powerful or clever or hilarious lines spoken by the actor usually originate with the playwright. The graceful or amusing gestures and movements may represent his contribution or the director's, often both. The beautiful clothing that the actor wears comes from the costumer. Even the performer's physical beauty may reflect his skill as a makeup designer more than the actor's actual appearance.

Specifically, then, what qualities does an audience member seek when evaluating an actor's work? Any attempt to answer such a question will stimulate great controversy among critics of acting, but perhaps the following qualities will serve as a point of departure.

1. TRUTHFULNESS

Such a criterion is abstract, subjective, and dangerous. For a critic of acting to base evaluation on the concept of truthfulness implies that he knows the truth. In realistic or representational drama, this factor may relate to believability or lifelikeness; in presentational drama, a naturalistic acting approach may be totally inappropriate. In either case, however, artistic truthfulness and the degree to which the actor achieves it distinguishes greatness from mediocrity.

Truth may be defined negatively as the absense of deceit, positively as what is in accordance with fact. In acting, the facts are the facts of humanity and the human condition, which the actor seeks to portray in artistic form. Truth in acting begins with the actor. He must believe in the rightness of his actions before his fellow performers or the audience have any chance to. Even so abstract an art as mime makes similar demands; two mimes can go through almost exactly the same motions, but the audience may believe one and not the other. All else being equal, the difference lies in the performer's own attitude toward his actions; his own belief, supported by his craft as an artist, can stimulate a comparable response in the audience. Audiences, after all, want desperately to believe everything happening on a stage; they feel frustrated and disappointed when they do not. In this respect, the actor has a very real advantage.

Legend has it that Polis, an Athenian actor of the fifth century B.C., once played a Greek monarch bereft by loss of a son. The actor's production circumstances didn't encourage realistic acting; Polis, like most Athenian actors then, wore a mask covering his entire head, heavy body padding, and an ornate costume. Yet Polis brought on stage with him the ashes of his own dead son, seeking to stimulate something within himself leading to a greater honesty in his portrayal. Other actors since then have used comparable, though usually less traumatizing, devices to stimulate their psyches.

2. THE DEMANDS OF THE ROLE

Roles vary widely as to the demands made on the actor playing them. The title role in *Hamlet* exhausts the talents of most actors, whereas the role of Reynaldo in Act II, Scene 1, of the same script makes minimal demands and offers minimal rewards. But length of role is not the only consideration. Hamlet is a longer role than Othello, but experienced actors usually find Othello the more difficult to perform and King Lear still more demanding. The emotional spectrum of roles are a matter of infinite variety, a factor critics should consider in evaluating an actor's work.

However difficult the role, the evaluator should consider how well the actor has integrated his efforts with the entire production. Such roles as Hamlet, Cyrano, Oedipus, Hedda Gabbler, and Medea of necessity dominate productions of those scripts but must not do so to the exclusion of all others. The overpowering star may succceed commercially; artistically he is suspect.

3. FLEXIBILITY

Over the course of a career, an actor plays many roles. The variety of the roles he plays offers a possible index to his worth, assuming he succeeds. Again, Laurence Olivier has had an exemplary career: his successes in Shakespeare and other classic roles have won him worldwide acclaim, but his equally successful performances in modern dramas, such as *The Entertainer, The Three Sisters,* and *Long Day's Journey into Night,* reveal a talent of rare flexibility, including the ability to succeed in both comic and serious drama.

Ultimately any such evaluation of artistic endeavor must be personal and subjective. The actor's work has affected you personally, or it has not. The audience member may, however, be affected by matters quite irrelevant to the creative work of the actor, such as the following:

a. THE ACTOR'S REPUTATION AS AN ACTOR

Only stars have this "problem." Having won substantial success in earlier roles, the actor is expected by his audience to achieve brilliance in every performance. In some cases, however, this expectation works to the actor's advantage; audiences may be predisposed to accept and applaud even the actor's mediocre work. This advantage does not last long; last season's clippings have little effect upon this season's work.

b. THE ACTOR'S REPUTATION AS A PERSON

Actors in recent years have grown increasingly active politically, and some audiences have taken them to task when they disagreed. Jane and Peter Fonda, for example, have alienated some of their fans by their political liberalism. Bob Hope and John Wayne have done the same with their conservatism. Perhaps it all evens out over the long run. An actor's personal life may also add to or detract from his following, which can become an important box-office consideration. That such matters are irrelevant to a performance seems axiomatic in an aesthetic sense, but life in the public eye can make strange demands.

103

c. Attractiveness

Physical charm or beauty often represents a valuable commercial commodity for the actor, just as it might in a dog show, but it hardly relates to the actor's artistry. The evaluator of acting must distinguish clearly between commercial appeal and aesthetic worth if his criticism is to be more than an index of popularity.

Conclusions

The future for professional actors remains somewhat grim, as supply will no doubt continue to exceed demand. Regional repertory companies attract more and more attention here and in Europe, and this configuration of work increases the potential for artistic excellence. Also, playwrights working with resident companies tend to involve the actors more in the actual creation of a script by testing early versions with them, revising with considerable input from the cast, and working as part of an artistic community.

Such innovations do not constitute mere faddism. The actor remains the essential element in the theatre. As such, he deserves primacy in all considerations as a production agency prepares for public performance. More sensible and productive actors' training programs hopefully will raise the level of performance in future years and enable the actor to approach his profession with the dignity and respect it deserves.

Chapter Five

☆

The Designers

"There is no excellent beauty that hath not some strangeness in the proportion."
—FRANCIS BACON, *Essays of Beauty*

LEGEND has it that a small, second-rate company once toured Ireland with a production of Marlowe's *The Tragical History of Doctor Faustus*. In a small town one evening, the play drew to its conclusion and the actor playing Faustus thundered through his last speech:

> *Ah, Faustus,*
> *Now hast thou but one bare hour to live,*
> *And then must be damned perpetually!*

and so on to the closing lines:

> *My God, my God, look not so fierce on me!*
> *Adders and serpents, let me breathe awhile!*
> *Ugly hell, gape not! Come not, Lucifer!*
> *I'll burn my books!—Ah, Mephistophilis!*

During the last four climactic lines, Faustus started to sink below the stage floor, by means of an elevatorlike trap, into red light suggesting the pits of hell. Unfortunately the trap stuck about three feet down, leaving Faustus's upper torso above stage level with literally no place to go. The audience greeted this development with stunned silence, until a beery voice from the top gallery bellowed out, "Hallelujah, boys, hell's full!"

Anyone working in the theatre for very long will amass a storehouse of such anecdotes about stage doors not open-

FIGURE 5-1. *The Fortune Theatre, one of the Elizabethan public theatres in competition with Shakespeare's company at the Globe.*

ing, moustaches coming off, costumes splitting, scenery collapsing, curtains refusing to open or close, light or sound effects coming at the wrong time, missing properties, and the like. These moments often offer great hilarity in retrospect, but at the time they are seldom amusing. The cast sees hundreds of hours of work destroyed, and audiences usually experience great discomfort as the company loses control of its production. Everyone anticipates a certain number of accidents during rehearsals, when they can be remedied, but there are no "out-takes" during production.

Such accidents indicate a considerable production responsibility for the designers and the technicians. More than just not making mistakes, however, designers and technicians can contribute richly to the success of a production. In the modern theatre, the design and execution of scenery, lighting, costumes, properties, makeup, and sound effects have grown into fully developed theatrical professions and specialties. Examination of each of these can expand the theatregoer's understanding and appreciation of the various designers' contributions to production in the theatre.

The Scenic Designer

The scenic designer's work has an effect both massive and subtle upon the audience in the traditional theatre. Considering scenery in the widest sense as those visual elements that define the space in which the theatrical event takes place—distinguished from theatre architecture in that they constitute temporary elements for a specific production—the following purposes commonly apply to most production situations.

1. *Definition of Space.* In traditional, realistic, proscenium theatre, a setting often delineates some specific locale in which the action of the play occurs. Modern plays often take place in a living room, for example, but playwrights have set their scripts almost everywhere: a cloudbank in heaven, Golgotha, Delphi, Cleopatra's throne room, the

Théâtre du Marais in Paris, a meadow, the Flavian Am-pitheatre, bars, brothels, bedrooms, Tara, streets, Mars, or hell. Even though the scenic designer may not attempt to delineate such locales realistically, he must bring a wide awareness of reality to any interpretation of such sites.

In any event, he must usually define the space in which the actors perform. In an arena production with the audi-ence surrounding the action, the scenic designer ordinarily uses very little traditional scenery, but the minimal elements used therefore take on even greater importance. In some cases, the designer may use no scenery at all; if the produc-tion takes place in a replica of Shakespeare's Globe Theatre, for example, or if a happening is staged in a bus depot or some other "found" space. Nevertheless, someone selects the space for the production, and that selection determines much of the production's eventual form and nature.

2. *Evocation of Mood.* The space designed for a produc-tion should appear visually appropriate to the events con-tained within it. In the simplest examples, living rooms, the characters' nature and the effects sought upon the audience by the designer determine the room's specific character-istics. *Who's Afraid of Virginia Woolf?,* for example, requires a very different type of environment than *Time Out for Ginger, The Glass Menagerie,* or *The Waltz of the Toreadors.* In short, the space must be designed in terms of a particular vision of a particular script. Designers might otherwise construct a single living-room set for all such scripts.

Designers seek to achieve these necessary distinctions and thus the appropriate audience response by using the tradi-tional visual elements: color, line, mass, space, and texture. Designers rarely design *Hamlet, Oedipus Rex,* or *Macbeth* in pastel pinks or greens; such color choices would seem inap-propriate to those scripts, although they might serve ad-mirably for *The Importance of Being Earnest* or a Restoration comedy. Color psychology thus constitutes a basic tool of the designer. So too, variations of line can support or de-tract from a production. Traditionally, crossed diagonal lines imply conflict; circles and quick curves support com-

108

edy (polka-dot clown costumes, for example); long, slow curves tend toward the sensuous and suggest the lines of the human body; tall verticals lead the eye toward the heavens, as exemplified by the Gothic arch. Rarely do designers use the elements so simply, but the subtle use of such elements can and does have emotional impact upon an audience, often below the level of awareness, and these elements can thus amplify the theatrical event.

3. *Focus of Attention.* By the very definition of the playing space, the designer focuses the audience's attention upon that space. Selective lighting, described later, further forces the audience to concentrate upon a specified area. But within the defined space, the designer, by his arrangement of elements, can give subspaces visual priority, especially in proscenium or three-quarter staging. The director often uses down center (the area closest to the audience and in the middle of the stage) for a play's most important scenes or those that he hopes to give the most impact. A designer often tries to assist by leaving this area uncluttered or by grouping furniture in such a way as to allow the director to emphasize specific actors and scenes. The director and the designer, therefore, must obviously coordinate their efforts.

4. *Amplification of the Theatrical Event.* By defining space, evoking mood, and focusing attention, the designer gives added dimension to the theatrical event. The contribution of stage scenery should be evaluated only in these terms. Very good scenery for one production might well appear absurd for another—even another production of the same script. Scenery in isolation has no meaning. Only as it contributes to a total production concept and execution do its values emerge.

THE SCENIC DESIGNER'S RELATIONSHIP WITH CO-WORKERS

As suggested earlier, the scenic designer works most closely with the director. They must share a mutual vision of the production from start to finish. More than mere courtesy demands such a relationship; the designer's arrangement of elements very definitely programs the actors into specific movement patterns. The designer may have carefully arranged movement potential that the director overlooks or does not care to use, or he may have restricted movement potential, but usually more subtle matters demand the attention of both. For a production of *Hamlet,* for example, the production staff must decide early whether the script depicts a weak-willed and vacillating young prince thrust into a situation beyond his capacities or, on the other hand, a man of action who seeks to confirm his suspicions before he sweeps to his revenge. Directors and designers should confer until they can agree on basic interpretations. Their conscious decisions should then permeate all elements of the production from casting to costume and property selection. If the production staff disagrees on such points, the eventual production runs a considerable risk of being an uneasy compromise. Certainly it will lack organic unity and coherence.

Similarly, if separate artists create the scenic and lighting designs, only close coordination can achieve unity. Selection of the color filters usually used on lighting instruments can substantially enhance or destroy a scenic designer's color scheme. The costume designer also must coordinate color, line, and period with the scenic designer, as must the personnel in charge of furniture and other properties. In most production companies, the final arbiter of any conflicts is the director.

THE SCENIC DESIGNER'S ALTERNATIVES AND RESTRICTIONS

Modern scenic designers face almost unlimited options when confronted by the varieties of design styles, script demands, and directorial visions. As in other aspects of the theatre, theorists and critics have assigned titles and categories to various approaches. As in the other elements, these categories merely attempt to describe; they do not cover all possibilities or options. Nevertheless such pigeonholing can illuminate some of the major options of the scenic designer.

Representationalism versus presentationalism, as in the case of the playwright, offers a point of departure. The designer first decides whether he should devise a setting that by being immediately recognizable to the audience offers the illusion of an actual place or whether the setting should attempt no such illusion and remain overtly theatrical. These do not represent mutually exclusive categories, and designers may mix styles within a production. Few designers attempt absolute realism, finding it neither desirable nor feasible. At best, they invite the audience to suspend its disbelief but not to believe that the locale on stage is actually what it seems. Designers work in various other styles (selective realism, expressionism, impressionism, surrealism, and so on), but usually their work lies along a spectrum of styles ranging from realism to theatricalism.

The director's vision of the production places definite parameters upon the designer's creation, but within those limits the designer still finds enormous creative opportunity. If the two disagree sharply, the designer must either bend to the director's desires or seek employment elsewhere. Excellence often demands negotiation in group endeavors.

The architecture of the theatre affects the designer's options to a large degree. First, he must consider the type of stage upon which his work will appear and the auditorium from which the audience will view it. If the script calls for more than one setting, storage space for the unused scenery must be available. Designers must check sight lines from the auditorium to ensure the audience can see all the playing area but not into the backstage area. Stage equipment, such as elevators, trap doors, flying equipment, lighting posi-

111

tions, doorways, and the like, often determine whether or not a particular design can function on a specific stage.

Budgetary considerations often frustrate designers. Materials and labor make up a major portion of most production expenses. The designer must work within the existing financial circumstances, and lack of funds may eliminate desirable but expensive materials and procedures. He may have hundreds of thousands of dollars available in the commercial theatre; he may have a few thousand or even hundred dollars in an educational or a community theatre. Low budgets test the designer's imagination, taste, and craft.

Within the restrictions of style, directorial vision, architecture, and budget, the designer sets out to create an environment for an action, a housing for an artistic event, and a visual contribution to that event.

REQUISITES FOR EXCELLENCE IN SCENIC DESIGN

Like other theatre artists, the scenic designer profits from wide experience in the theatre in all capacities that familiarizes him with all aspects of production. Experience in acting and directing offer especially valuable insights, because actors and directors will use his settings most directly. Personal experience of the problems of traffic patterns, movement potential, furniture arrangements, bringing crowds on stage, and similar concerns usually increases the designer's appreciation of these matters.

The ability to envision a production from reading the script constitutes a major talent for successful designers, just as for directors. This ability stems from wide theatrical experience, from both seeing and staging productions. The beginning script-reader often encounters great frustration in this regard, but the designer must draw upon all his

112

imaginative resources and translate them into both practical and aesthetic terms to create scenery of exellence.

Obviously the outstanding designer develops a high sense of visual beauty, harmony, proportion, color, mass, form, line, and so on, comparable to that of the easel painter or the sculptor but considered in the unique terms of stage design. Unlike the solitary artist, the designer must always remember the communal and pragmatic restrictions demanded by the theatre. Somewhat like an architect, he should be familiar with the load-bearing capacities of the various materials with which he works, lest his scenery collapse of its own weight. And like any builder, he should have a considerable curiosity about new methods and better materials.

Above all, as has already been implied, the scenic designer must willingly subordinate his work to the entire production. Although he must serve as his own most severe critic and, like any artist, must insist upon excellence in his own work, he must perceive that scenic design functions only in conjunction with other theatrical elements. Artistic temperament can contribute to excellence when it passionately seeks excellence, but it defeats itself and becomes self-indulgence when it disallows others to do their best work as well.

Thus training for a career in scenic design properly begins with a wide theatrical background. The designer profits as well, from work in the graphic arts and sculpture. This training contributes the required craftsmanship. In addition, the work drawings and blueprints for the actual scenery demand drafting ability, for the most ethereal and aesthetic of designs must translate via working drawings into specific sizes and grades of lumber, plaster, plastic, cloth, and other materials. The scenic designer often needs academic research ability in order to find the information necessary for specific settings. For example, not many plays take place on or near bridges, but if a designer attempts *A*

113

View from the Bridge, Luv, or *Winterset,* he will surely find some knowledge of bridge construction mandatory. Exterior scenes frequently demand an awareness of appropriate vegetation. Plays such as *Androcles and the Lion* and Greek plays may lead the designer to a study of classical architecture.

THE CONTEMPORARY SITUATION FOR THE SCENIC DESIGNER

In the professional theatre, designers of all kinds, including scenic designers, are members of the United Scenic Artists, which has offices in most major cities. Its membership includes scenic designers, scenic artists, costume designers, lighting designers, and others. The union's jurisdiction includes legitimate theatre, motion pictures, and television.

The functions of the USA include the establishment of fees for union designers, negotiation with employers to secure the best possible wages and fringe benefits, and representation of the union designers to obtain additional benefits.

One obtains membership in the USA by passing a very rigorous examination. Usually, depending upon the specific classification of membership, the prospective member completes a home project (much like a take-home examination) demonstrating his knowledge and skill. The written examination, which constitutes the second part of the application, may cover designing, sketching, lighting, drafting, geometry, mathematics, history of art and drama, and scenic painting skills. Although many applicants fail the examination on the first attempt, they may retake it as often as they wish, and an applicant may serve as an apprentice union member to gain the necessary experience.

Once the examination has been passed, the designer becomes a union member and can get in touch with directors and producers. As a union member, the designer enjoys

114

professional acceptance, and appointments become much easier to obtain. For this reason, substantial initiation fees are charged: $550 for a design director, $300 for a scenic designer or scenic artist, and $150 for a lighting or costume designer. In addition, a $50 nonrefundable examination fee is assessed, and union dues are paid annually.

Designers may demand substantial fees, however. Figure 5-2 presents minimum fees for various design configurations as of September 1976. Note that theatre seating capacity (and therefore potential income) is considered on a sliding scale, as are the number of settings, the number of costumes, the number of scenes, and the length of the show's run. Although many students of the modern theatre suggest that unionization has inflated production costs excessively, others suggest that most of the time the theatre artist in the commercial theatre is not working at all and therefore must receive substantial payment in order to survive, let alone prosper. Another argument grows out of the relative percentage of a total production budget going to performers, directors, and designers as opposed to that allotted to rent, stage hands, and similar expenses. While exact figures vary from production to production, the theatre artist coming to the commercial theatre from an educational or community theatre background will experience severe shock at the fiscal proportions of the commercial budget. Interested students will find the history of theatrical unions a challenging and revealing study.

The employment circumstances for educational theatre designers vary considerably. In small high schools, one person may take charge of all theatre activity, along with other, nontheatrical duties. Under such circumstances, the director–designer comprises the entire staff and supervises all elements of production. One person, no matter how talented or motivated, can rarely achieve excellence when spread so thin. One finds comparable circumstances in many small colleges; the "one-man department" in theatre sadly remains very much in evidence.

115

MINIMUM DESIGN FEES EFFECTIVE 9/1/75 - 9/1/76

SET DESIGNER RATES

THEATRE SEATING CAPACITY	MINIMUM RATES			
	First Set (or basic unit set)	Next Set or phase	Next 4 Sets or phases	More than 6 Sets or phases
Over 1000 seats	$1,650.00	$550.00	$302.50	$181.50
500 - 999 seats	$1,375.00	$440.00	Additional Sets or phases $242.00 each	
300 - 499 seats	$1,100.00	$211.20	$90.75 each	
200 - 299 seats	$825.00	$150.70	$42.35 each	
199 or less seats	$495.00	$60.50	$24.20 each	

COSTUME DESIGNER RATES

THEATRE SEATING CAPACITY	MINIMUM RATES			
	NUMBER OF COSTUMES 10 or less	11 - 20	21 - 30	31 plus
Over 1000 seats	$1,100.00	$54.45ea.	$36.30ea.	$30.25ea.
500 - 999 seats	$1045.00	$42.35ea.	$30.25ea.	$18.15ea.
300 - 499 seats	$935.00	$30.25ea.	Additional Costumes $18.15 ea.	
200 - 299 seats	$605.00	$24.20ea.	Additional Costumes $12.00 ea.	
199 or less seats	$440.00	$6.05 ea.	Additional Costumes $6.05 ea.	

FIGURE 5-2. *Recent minimum design fees for the commercial designer. Permission from United Scenic Artists.*

LIGHTING DESIGNER RATES

THEATRE SEATING CAPACITY	MINIMUM RATES	
	Single Set	Multiple Scenes or Phases
Over 1000 seats	$1,100.00	$1,375.00
500 - 999 seats	$935.00	$1,100.00
300 - 499 seats	$770.00	$852.50
200 - 299 seats	$660.00	$765.00
199 or less seats	$495.00	$550.00

MINIMUM ROYALTIES PER WEEK FOR ALL DESIGNERS

THEATRE SEATING CAPACITY	First five weeks	Fifth to 16th week	From 16th week on
Over 1000 seats	$40.00	$50.00	$60.00
500 - 999 seats	$30.00	$40.00	$50.00
300 - 499 seats	$25.00	$35.00	$50.00
200 - 299 seats	$20.00	$30.00	$45.00
199 or less seats	$15.00	$25.00	$40.00

117

Many junior colleges, some high schools, and most colleges, however, hire a separate staff member, usually called the *technical director,* to supervise staging elements. This person may serve simultaneously as construction supervisor and designer and may also teach classes in technical theatre. Such a position obviously improves upon the "one-man department," but if the technical director must also supervise stage lighting, makeup, and costumes, demands can become excessive.

Larger departments often hire several technical specialists in order to delegate responsibilities more equitably. One or more scenic designers, a technical director with assistants for various areas, and separate costume and lighting designers constitute a traditional deployment of personnel. Such a configuration can foster the best work being done in educational theatre today, assuming, as always, talent, motivation, and expertise.

Salary ranges in education vary with academic degree, training, professorial rank, experience, geographic location, and administrative attitudes. A beginning high-school teacher might expect $8,000 annually; a full professor at a major university might receive three or four times that much. Educational designers often affiliate with the American Theatre Association, but they may also join an organization specifically for theatre technicians, the United States Institute of Theatre Technology, which holds annual meetings and publishes a highly regarded journal.

CREATIVE PROCEDURES FOR THE SCENIC DESIGNER

Again, individual variation typifies designers in their work, but the following is a normal sequence.

1. SCRIPT ANALYSIS

Having read the script carefully, the designer meets with the director to discuss the specific demands of the script, the production style, the budget, and all other relevant matters. At this point, the designer may make a substantial impact upon the production concept by offering alternative design concepts to the director. These meetings should continue until the director and the designer have a common vision of production intentions.

2. ROUGH SKETCHES

The designer now begins to put his concepts in tangible form, usually as rough perspective sketch, a floor plan, or even a model. Again, considerable give-and-take can occur as the designer and the director move toward agreement.

FIGURE 5-3A. *A rough sketch by the author for an intended production of Lanford Wilson's* The Hot l Baltimore. *No precise scale is intended. Rather, the sketch is an approximation of scenic elements.*

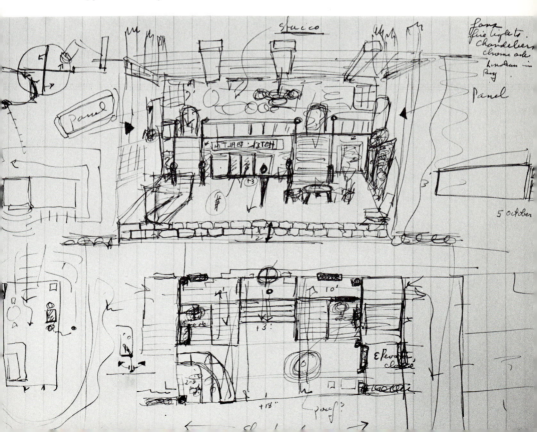

3. FLOOR PLAN AND SIDE ELEVATIONS

The designer may next convert the rough sketches into a more detailed and accurate scale plan to insure his concept will fit the specific space. A side elevation or cross section of the stage serves the same function with regard to vertical dimension. Designers may draft these plans simultaneously with the following.

4. PERSPECTIVE DRAWINGS AND/OR MODELS

Many designers prepare a scale perspective drawing of the setting(s) to depict their intentions graphically. Other designers prepare and construct a model of the setting, preferring to deal in three-dimensional form from the outset

FIGURE 5-3B. *A designer's floor plan for a production of* The Hot l Baltimore. *Figures preceded by a plus sign indicate height above the stage floor in inches; curve diameters are given to facilitate construction and layout. By the author.*

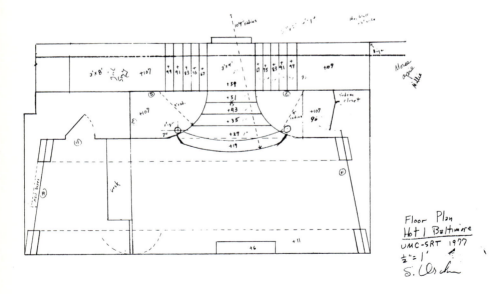

FIGURE 5-4A. *A perspective drawing of* Scapino *as produced by the Young Vic in London. By employing perspective drawing techniques, the designer approximated closely the eventual setting. Note the different arrangement of elements indicated in Figure 3-2, which includes the floor plan for the touring show. By permission of holder of rights of* Scapino, *the Dramatic Publishing Company, 4150 North Milwaukee Avenue, Chicago, Ill. 60641.*

of the design project. Usually the designer attempts to solve problems of color, line, and mass at this time. By putting his solutions in graphic, tangible form, he facilitates communication with construction personnel, actors, and other theatre artists. For that reason, some designers prefer to prepare both models and perspective drawings.

5. BLUEPRINTS OR WORKING DRAWINGS

If the director has approved the designs thus far, the designer converts all scenic elements into blueprints to be used by construction crews and supervisors. If the design

FIGURE 5-4B. *A model setting for* Hamlet. *By working in three dimensions in a model, the designer encounters many of the same considerations that he will in the actual setting. Permission from the designer, Henry Tharp.*

FIGURE 5-4C. *The same* Hamlet *model viewed from above, giving much the same impression as a floor plan. Permission from the designer, Henry Tharp.*

FIGURE 5-4D. *The Hamlet setting in actual production during Hamlet's death. Permission from the designer, Henry Tharp.*

requires especially complex painting, additional drawings may be made for those elements. These drawings require great accuracy if costly and time-consuming errors are to be avoided.

6. Supervision of Construction

In larger operations, the designer turns the working drawings over to the construction supervisors, who may confer with him in the event of difficulty. In most situations, the designer checks periodically on the progress of construction. If he is in a one-man technical operation, he himself supervises and assists in construction.

7. Setup of the Scenery

Erecting the scenery for the run of a show may require the services of the designer, especially if the show has multiple sets or complex elements. If the production will run in repertory, or if it must be taken down and reset for any reason, the designer may wish to oversee this operation as well.

123

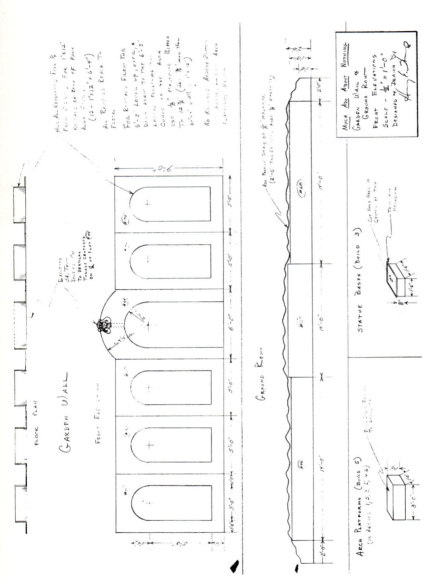

FIGURE 5-4E AND F. *Typical working drawings. These blueprints are used by scenic construction personnel for the actual building of the scenery. Permission from the designer, Henry Tharp.*

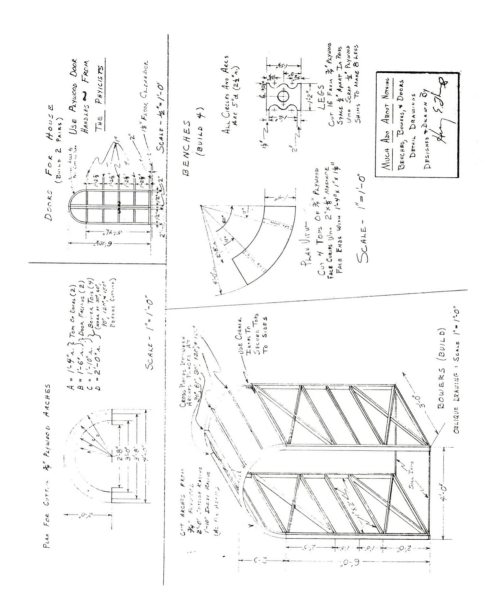

8. Strike

At the end of the show's run of performances, crews clear all scenery from the stage. The commercial theatre must often discard such scenery for financial reasons. In the educational and community theatres, reusable elements are often salvaged for future shows. The designer does not usually supervise this operation, unless so requested.

EVALUATION OF STAGE SCENERY

In evaluating stage scenery, the audience member finds that he can often separate the designer's work somewhat more easily from the other theatre artists' contributions. Physical objects make up scenery, and the audience member can thus evaluate the concrete manifestations of the designer's intentions with seemingly more assurance than he can the actors', the director's, or the playwright's.

In evaluating stage scenery, however, the audience member should avoid the temptation to judge it in isolation or out of the context of the total production. The reader will already have deduced that how well stage scenery achieves the functions listed earlier determines its quality, but he should remember to apply those functions to the particular production of a specific script rather than considering the scenery as a separate entity.

Even in so relatively simple a matter as defining the playing space, designers find wide latitude. In modern, realistic drama, designers may restrict the action to behind the proscenium arch, and the actors make no overt contact with the audience. In musical comedy, such as *A Chorus Line,* action is similarly restricted primarily to the stage, but the cast frequently directs musical numbers directly to the audience. In even more blatantly theatrical productions, such as *Hair* or *Godspell,* the cast may come off the stage into the audience for direct confrontation, and the setting should assist

126

FIGURE 5-5A. *The setting for* A Midsummer Night's Dream *as staged by Max Reinhardt in 1905. This highly successful production carried naturalism to extremes by modern standards. Permission from the Max Reinhardt Archive, State University of New York—Binghamton.*

FIGURE 5-5B. *Dancers in the Reinhardt* A Midsummer Night's Dream. *Again, note the attempted photographic naturalism of the setting. Permission from the Max Reinhardt Archive, State University of New York—Binghamton.*

the varying degrees of direct performer–audience interaction.

So too with the evocation of mood. The designer for an Ibsen drama may well focus the visual attention of the audience strictly upon the stage, whereas the designer for *Hair* purposely blurs the division between stage and auditorium, facilitating the looseness of the action by manifesting in scenery the unconstrained nature of the script. In the latter case, the mood of the setting, like the overall mood of the script, decries traditional or logical structure.

In focusing audience attention, the designer may wish at times to rivet audience attention upon a single performer, or he may at other times spread the focus to include the entire theatre, both stage and auditorium. Again, the director, the designer, and the other theatre artists must have a single goal in mind and must coordinate their efforts to achieve that goal.

Scenic quality, therefore, revolves around the question of whether or not the scenery has amplified the specific theatrical event as conceived and executed. Three separate productions of *A Midsummer Night's Dream* exemplify the matter of specificity of production intentions. Max Reinhardt's production in 1905 offers the most traditional approach, especially in the forest scenes, realistically depicted. In 1970 Peter Brook staged the same script for the Royal Shakespeare Company in an extremely nontraditional manner and won worldwide acclaim. The Tyrone Guthrie production in 1972 resembled neither of the other two, yet achieved a very high artistic level. In staging three excellent productions of the same script, three companies approached and solved their scenic problems in three totally distinct ways. Each setting, although eminently appropriate to each company's specific production intentions, would have been useless to the other companies. Critics of stage scenery simply cannot safely judge scenery out of context.

Nevertheless traditional concerns of graphic-art evaluation often relate to the scenic designer's work, especially in

FIGURE 5-5C. A Midsummer Night's Dream *as staged by Peter Brook for the Royal Shakespeare Company in 1970. This production, which won worldwide acceptance, differed sharply from traditional Shakespearean staging.*

FIGURE 5-5D. A Midsummer Night's Dream *as staged in 1972 at the Tyrone Guthrie Theatre in Minneapolis. An excellent production in a remarkably different conception from those of Reinhardt and the Royal Shakespeare Company. Permission from the Tyrone Guthrie Theatre.*

proscenium staging. These include balance, rhythm, emphasis, harmony, color coordination, and so on. Scenery does not always require beauty in the usual sense, but it should attract the eye and interest the viewer. The concept of variety in unity and vice versa challenges all artists. Certainly the director, the painter, the dancer, the sculptor, the architect, and the stage designer seek a unity expressive of intention but containing variations interesting to the viewer. Such concerns complicate the creation of art, and the evaluation of art is equally complex, calling for deep insights in the creative process.

SUMMARY

Future developments in scenic design will follow as technicians and designers attune themselves to technological innovations. The use of mixed media steadily increases. Technicians continue to discover lighter, cheaper, and simpler materials for use in the theatre. Designers have experimented with laser beams to form gigantic scenic holograms, and enormous video screens appeared in the British National Theatre's production of Tom Stoppard's *Jumpers*. Only the imagination and the artistry of the scenic designer limit the future.

Overall, modern theatre tends toward less traditional scenery on stage and a return to the dominance of the actor. But at the same time, technical elements have gained increased respect in the pursuit of excellence. Modern theatre artists attempt to combine all visual elements into an organic, unified production concept of increasing sophistication. Modern audiences reap the benefits of such effort.

The Lighting Designer

As the name implies, the lighting designer conceives and supervises all elements of stage illumination. Like the scene

130

designer's, his work affects the production by simultaneously massive and subtle means. He first makes visible all other visual elements of the theatre, and his illumination usually covers the stage from side to side and from front to back. He often, however, seeks effects occurring below the audience's conscious level but nevertheless with potential for eliciting considerable emotional response.

Stage lighting as we know it today has grown increasingly more sophisticated since Edison's invention of the incandescent light bulb in 1879, its first use in a theatre in 1881, and the considerably increased efficiency of the light bulb by 1919. Modern lighting designers can choose the amount, the direction, the color, and the specific nature of the light illuminating the acting area, giving him a near-infinite combination of effects.

Again, the director's overall production concept unifies multiple efforts. The director usually describes his goals to the lighting designer, giving him aesthetic freedom within restrictions. The scenery's nature and placement frequently further modify the lighting designer's work. In most theatres, the lighting designer begins work only after the scene designer had planned the setting. As previously noted, the costumer and the lighting designer must coordinate their work for best results.

In the smaller theatre operations, as we have seen, one person may direct and design all elements of a production. For this discussion, we will assume the separation of lighting design from the other production elements.

THE LIGHTING DESIGNER'S ALTERNATIVES AND RESTRICTIONS

Because he deals with electricity in its most practical applications, the lighting designer often finds that other theatre artists do not completely understand his work, any more than the average citizen comprehends applied electricity. Moreover, the lighting designer deals with complex and costly equipment to achieve his goals. The nature of light carries with it its own seemingly mystical qualities, further complicating matters. Stage lighting weds the most aesthetic of artistic considerations with a most complex and unforgiving science.

Usually the lighting designer's first restrictions are the directorial vision. Hopefully the director understands the lighting designer's procedures to some degree; at the very least, he should understand the working circumstances. Technical operations of all sorts offer innumerable problems, and the director should at the very least be willing to listen to difficulties as they come up.

Limitations of equipment most often complicate the lighting designer's work. Obviously the number of available lighting instruments limits what a lighting designer can achieve. Similarly the type of lighting instruments at his command will affect his potential achievement. Spotlights vary as to design and function, from lekos (using plano-convex lenses and parabolic reflectors) for lighting from considerable distances to Fresnels (using stepped lenses and spherical reflectors) for closer work. Designers use various sorts of general lighting instruments, such as floodlights, to supply general illumination over large areas such as a backdrop, as well as specialized instruments such as scenic projectors, follow spots, strip lights for lighting cycloramas, and the like. Each instrument varies in wattage, 250–1500 watts being most common.

Secure arrangements for hanging lighting instruments, which in combination make up considerable weight, affect a designer's options. Theatres vary widely in this respect; the better ones have openings in the auditorium ceiling for instruments and pipes (called *battens*) over the acting area to support instruments there. Many designers employ side lighting from the wings, but space must be available there for this technique. Whatever arrangement the designer uses, he must have support and current for each instrument.

132

FIGURE 5-6A. *The auditorium of the University Theatre at Southern Illinois University—Edwardsville. Note the definite rake of the auditorium, facilitating sight lines, and unusual box seats at the left. The numerous slots in the ceiling greatly assist in the lighting of the stage, from which this photo was taken. Author's photograph.*

Presupposing the above, the control system or dimmer board further affects the eventual design. Each light or group of lights is usually connected by circuitry to a dimming device of a limited size; this dimmer enables the board operator to determine the intensity of each lighting instrument. Obviously the number of circuits available will determine the maximum number of instruments employed in a show. The use of an interconnecting panel, comparable to a telephone switchboard, increases flexibility. Most theatres have such a device. A unit used in only one scene can thus be disconnected, and another unit can be "patched" into that circuit for later use. Such techniques require the meticulous coordination of all concerned.

Dimmer capacity determines how many instruments technicians can connect to a single circuit. A 6000-watt dimmer can control a dozen 500-watt instruments, for example. Overloading a circuit trips circuit breakers, blows fuses, or

133

burns up the dimmer, the light booth, or the theatre. Stage lighting is no place for the dilettante; safety regulations and equipment expense demand knowledgeable procedure. In this facet of theatrical production, an error can literally be a matter of life and death.

REQUISITES FOR EXCELLENCE IN STAGE LIGHTING

Successful stage-lighting design requires a visual sense comparable to that needed for scenic design but with vastly different specific manifestations. Stage lighting illuminates something already existent; actors, costumes, scenery, properties, makeup, and so on. Thus the lighting designer often creates in response to another artist's previous creation. Although he deals with all the traditional elements of visual art, light has the unique qualities of fluidity, which often

FIGURE 5-6B. *The ceiling of the University Theatre auditorium at the University of Missouri–Columbia. In this theatre, only a single lighting slot is available in the auditorium ceiling. Technicians have rigged additional battens from which to suspend lighting instruments. Author's photograph.*

FIGURE 5-6C. *A modern control console. In the foreground one sees the lighting control panel with banks of switches and faders, which control dimmers located elsewhere. In the background is the sound-control panel with two rack-mounted tape recorders. The window at the left overlooks the stage (see Figure 6-2), allowing the operators to observe the play in performance without disturbing the audience. Author's photograph.*

FIGURE 5-6D. *A modern interconnecting or patch panel for lighting control, by which various circuits are connected to various dimmers on the control panel, allowing greater flexibility in lighting control. Author's photograph.*

gives the lighting designer an opportunity to make unique aesthetic contributions to a production. Stage lighting rarely comes to rest and remains static any more than actors do for long periods of time. Rather the lighting often changes, altering focus and mood according to the show's demands. A successful lighting design counterpoints the script as visual music.

The lighting designer obviously needs a strong background in the technical and scientific aspects of his work. Basic optics, practical electrical ability, and the science of color are constant concerns. As lighting controls and instruments become increasingly sophisticated, so must the designer. Computer memory banks for lighting control increase in number and complexity. Quartz iodine lamps (bulbs) have replaced many tungsten-filament lamps. Remote-control devices proliferate. And each innovation forces the designer to reexamine his operational procedures.

The lighting designer must cooperate with other contributing theatre artists and often sees his work modified by others' contributions. The prima donna lighting designer has no more place in the theatre than does the excessively temperamental artist of any kind.

As always, the lighting designer's training appropriately begins with experience in all areas of the theatre. The lighting designer who has never directed or who looks upon actors as unfortunate complications in his work has a reductive vision of the theatre and rarely achieves excellence.

Beyond the scientific study demanded by their art, lighting designers find that they must continually examine and compare all available lighting equipment because quality control in equipment manufacture varies widely. Continual marketing of new equipment makes this an unending study. At each convention of the American Theatre Association or the United States Institute of Theatre Technology, for example, lighting companies display their latest developments. The successful designer must keep up with the technological innovations that make his artistry possible.

Because lighting technicians seem to work in a field remote from their fellow theatre artists, they sometimes seem to remove themselves from basic production concerns. The excellent lighting designer, of course, does not fall victim to this fallacy; he must above all remain sensitive to the production's goals and demands and employ his unique creative materials to achieve and amplify those goals. Although his tools and methods may seem scientific, his goals must remain aesthetic, and his contribution supports and amplifies the work of his fellow artists.

THE CONTEMPORARY SITUATION FOR THE LIGHTING DESIGNER

The circumstances of the professional or commercial lighting designer are the same as those described in the section titled "The Contemporary Situation for the Scenic Designer." One finds the Broadway lighting designer, as well as those who light road shows and Off-Broadway productions, working with startlingly antiquated materials and instruments in many cases. Only lately has modern equipment begun to be used on Broadway. Nevertheless, lighting of unparalleled excellence is the hallmark of the Broadway production.

In the educational and avocational theatre, lighting designers rarely specialize to the exclusion of other related activities. In a university theatre, the lighting designer often holds professorial rank, with all the resulting implications. He usually teaches as well as designs, and only in the largest of theatre programs does he teach only lighting. Smaller colleges and secondary schools rarely have stage-lighting specialists. More commonly the theatre technician must attend to a wide range of technical responsibilities. Community theatres often press into service anyone with a basic understanding of electrical circuits, although notable exceptions occur throughout the nation.

137

The formation of the United States Institute of Theatre Technology, with its journal, *Theatre Design and Technology,* and the increasing circulation of *Theatre Crafts,* a publication devoted almost exclusively to technical theatre, has helped upgrade the status of the nonprofessional theatre technician. In the past, this theatre technician frequently found himself a second-class citizen in the theatre, one called upon to do onerous and boring work behind the scenes and frequently selected only because he couldn't act. This reductive view of technical theatre negates excellence, but an increasing respect for the technician's contributions has now spread widely in the profession.

CREATIVE PROCEDURES FOR THE LIGHTING DESIGNER

Faced with a new production, the lighting designer proceeds at first much as does a scenic designer, first familiarizing himself with the script and then meeting with the director to analyze the specific demands and style sought in the intended production. After the first step, however, the lighting designer proceeds differently. Obtaining a floor plan from the scenic designer, he begins drafting a light plot, such as the one in Figure 5-7. This plot outlines an intention, indicating where the designer intends to position his lighting instruments. The director should understand light plots sufficiently to evaluate the design at this point. Concurrently with the light plot, the lighting designer plans instrument circuitry for the dimmer board and the requisite patch-panel connections. Using these documents, he then evolves a rough cue sheet, listing what changes in lighting occur during the production, when they occur, which instruments and dimmers will be involved, and the speed at which the changes should occur. Board operators usually revise and rewrite their cue sheets many times before a show opens. Rarely does reality equal expectation.

138

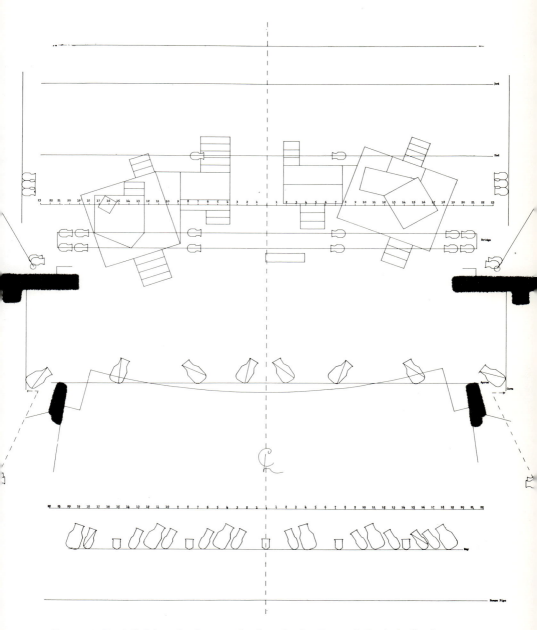

FIGURE 5-7. *A lighting plot for a production of* John Brown's Body *by Stephen Vincent Benet. Platforms and step units are indicated on the floor plan, as are the locations of the various lighting instruments. The heavy lines indicate the proscenium arch and the auditorium walls. Permission from the designer, Arthur Alvis.*

With the director's approval of the work thus far, the lighting crew hang the instruments in their desired locations, connect them to the dimmer board and patch panel, focus them upon the appropriate area of the stage, and place appropriate color filters in each unit. This work frequently involves quite strenuous labor; crew members often find themselves atop thirty-foot ladders wrestling 60 or 70 pound, 1500-watt spotlights into position.

Although not always used, a "dry tech" or "cue-to-cue" rehearsal with the director tests the design thus far. Typically the director and the designers set the intensities or levels of illumination, correct the focusing if necessary, check colors, and run through the show from change to change, or cue to cue. The length and nature of such rehearsals has made holding them without the actors an increasingly common practice.

Full-scale technical rehearsals traditionally constitute the next step, with all production elements approximating performance conditions but subject to change, somewhat like an intersquad scrimmage. Successful and efficient technical rehearsals depend largely upon the coordinating abilities of the director and the designers and the degree to which the crews have adequately prepared themselves. At this point, the actors go through the entire show, but the technical staff may ask them to repeat a segment until the technical elements coordinate with the stage action. Depending upon the complexity of the technical matters, three to five such rehearsals should solidify most of the procedures.

Hopefully all technical matters smooth out, the nuances clarify for every move, and after several runthroughs (uninterrupted rehearsals) in which all elements are rehearsed very much as they have been planned for performance, the production can open for the public.

Because mechanical devices wear out, lamps burn out, dimmers corrode, and color filters fade, technicians must make periodic checks during the run to prevent malfunction during performance. This procedure varies widely

140

from theatre to theatre. For example, some use lamp charts to record how many hours a particular lamp has burned. Because manufacturers list the life expectancy for any given type of lamp, light crews can replace them before they burn out. In less organized operations, the light crew simply hopes that they won't burn out during performance on the premise that no amount of planning can substitute for dumb luck. This philosophy has ruined a great many performances.

EVALUATION OF STAGE LIGHTING

Stage lighting facilitates the audience's seeing, recognizing, and appreciating the action portrayed on the stage. As an important visual production element, lighting also has the previously mentioned functions of stage scenery. The extent to which lighting achieves these several functions determines its success or failure.

1. SEEING THE ACTION.

Obviously the audience must perceive the work of the actors and the other theatre artists. Scenes rarely play in total darkness except for special effects, as in *Black Comedy* or *Remains to Be Seen*. The practice of darkening the auditorium and lighting only the stage originated only in the past hundred years, since the advent of electric light. Lighting only the playing area facilitates audience concentration, of course, and audience decorum has improved markedly as a secondary benefit.

The lighting designer first seeks to make the action visible to the degree appropriate to the production. Some theatre artists feel that comedy calls for a higher level of illumination than serious drama, but in any genre an underlit stage strains audience concentration, and actors also seem much harder to hear and understand in dim light.

141

2. RECOGNIZING THE ACTION.

In realistic staging, light should appear to come from recognizable sources, literal scenic elements such as torches, oil lamps, fireplaces, windows, or household lights. Each of these apparent light sources emits light of a different quality and amount, and the lighting designer usually attempts to match the quality and amount of the stage illumination with that of the apparent source. Sunlight and moonlight in exterior scenes vary widely with time of day, climate, locale, and surroundings. The designer seeks to increase credulity and verisimilitude with his design of exterior as well as interior scenes.

Recognition also implies the use of form-revealing light, employing the artistic principles of chiaroscuro. Artists have long noted that the most form-revealing light falls from above and to one side of an object, approximately 45° in elevation and 45° to the side. Sunlight most commonly strikes objects in nature in this way. We have thus grown accustomed to perceiving form under these conditions. Nevertheless for years footlights were commonly employed in theatres, with the light striking the actors' faces from below and in front, a practice rarely used today.

3. APPRECIATING THE ACTION.

This function of stage lighting involves more relative and subjective concerns. Here again, the lighting designer seeks to predict the audience response to a certain set of visual stimuli. Here again, the designer seeks to increase audience appreciation by the manipulation of the elements under his control.

Modern lighting practices have blurred the distinctions between stage lighting and scenery. Even beams of light, visible in dust in the air over the stage, can and have become important visual elements. But even in a more traditional production, one in which light does not seek to call attention to itself, the amount, color, and quality of stage lighting subliminally affects the audience and their reception of the work presented. In this century, as stage lighting developed and playwrights grew increasingly aware of its enormous potential, the stage directions included in published scripts have grown increasingly explicit. The final scene of Anouilh's *The Waltz of the Toreadors,* for example, calls for a slowly fading sun as the General's hopes similarly fade. Shakespeare had no opportunity for lighting control in the Globe Theatre, but one need only read the opening scenes of *Hamlet, Macbeth, Julius Caesar,* and *A Midsummer Night's Dream* to see what a lighting designer can add to a production.

Other Designers: Costumes, Properties, Makeup, and Sound

Just as scenic and lighting designers can contribute enormously to audience reaction to a production, other theatrical artists have comparable potential. Similarly each of the other designers may have greater or lesser effect, depending upon the demands of the specific script and the specific directorial vision of it. So too, each of the other designers must integrate his work into a unified whole, combining it with the work of others, guided by the overall production concept.

STAGE COSTUMING

The old adage "clothes make the man," like most clichés, contains a nugget of truth. Clothing's immense emotional power can make it one of the best nerve tonics in the world. Clothing is literally the scenery all of us wear as we go about our daily pursuits. Like scenery, clothing projects an image.

143

We select that image two or three times a day from available resources. Assuming you're wearing something while you read this, how would you describe *your* intended image?

Because a stage costume should express the character's personality, costuming becomes an important part of the overall concept of a production. Stage costuming should in fact seek goals comparable to those of stage scenery previously described by expressing character, being capable of appreciation by the audience, assisting the actor in his work, and relating organically to the entire production.

The stage costumer faces unique problems in translating the production concept into clothing; the designs must fit a particular actor, no matter what his size or physical distinctions, and the costumes must survive continual, often violent, action. Further, costumers design groups of costumes, not just sets of individual ones, and the need to establish relationships between the characters creates continual concern. An obvious example occurs in *Romeo and Juliet,* in which great numbers of Montagues and Capulets appear on stage, designers often use contrasting color schemes to help the audience distinguish between them. Similarly costumers may use line, silhouette, or texture to achieve harmonies and contrasts. The costumer and the director may or may not choose to costume the cast in historically accurate clothing. If they do so, the costumer's research abilities may prove valuable.

Production companies with limited resources may choose to borrow or rent costumes rather than design and construct them, a process usually saving time and effort rather than money. More commonly the costumers, like most designers, move from script analysis to directorial meetings to sketches and plans to actual construction. Whether the producers borrow, rent, or construct costumes, they must make selections from available resources, guided as always by economic considerations, aesthetic principles, and production concept.

In the modern theatre, costuming ranges from everyday

clothing, frequently the only requirement for contemporary drama, to the lavish and spectacular costumes of major concern and appeal in musical comedy or historical pageantry. Even in productions featuring or using nudity, such as *Oh, Calcutta!*, *Hair,* or *Let My People Come,* the actors have costumes to take off. (A totally nude production could dispense with the costumers but might require extra makeup supervision.) Like the other designers and technicians, the stage costumer has attained increasing prestige in the modern theatre.

Costumers, like all theatre artists and perhaps all human beings, run the risk of overspecialization and forgetting to put their work in perspective. The Broadway director Robert Lewis offers an example:

> I'm fond of telling a story about the costume designer of *Brigadoon,* which I directed. The show had played New Haven and we then went on to Boston to open on Monday night. With very little time to set up we were terrified that things were not going to go well technically. The curtain went up on the first set, a small scene of two fellows lost in a forest, and it went along all right. The curtain came down on that scene and then there was a walk-over scene in front of the curtain in which the "merry villagers" come on waking up after having been asleep for a hundred years. As they came across the stage, the crew was setting up the next big scene behind the curtain, which was the village of MacConnachy Square. The orchestra was playing while the villagers sang as they went across the stage. It was a continuous scene; as they sang, "Come ye everywhere, to the fair," the curtain did not go up; it just stayed there. It was a terrifying moment! I was standing in the back and I grabbed choreographer Agnes DeMille's arm, breaking it only slightly. The conductor couldn't stop the orchestra because it was a continuous scene; the people behind the curtain were already singing—you could hear them clearly. Still it didn't go up. Then, slowly, the people behind gradually got discouraged and their voices began to fade away. Now, of the people in front, those who were near either side, just sneaked off;

145

those in the center had too far to go—they were trapped. Then finally, after an eternity, with the number half over, the curtain went up with a jerk. A few of the chorus were still singing and dancing a little, some were just standing around, still others were seated on the floor—the whole thing looked like the Edinburgh subway! In addition, at the same time that the front curtain went up the backdrop, on which the village of MacConnachy Square was painted, went up too, revealing the back wall of the Colonial Theatre in Boston. It was at this moment that the costume designer rushed up to me, grabbed my arm and said, "That chorus girl has the wrong socks on again!" Now *that* is specialization!

STAGE PROPERTIES

Theatre artists usually define properties as all items of furniture, ornament, or decoration on a stage setting, plus any object handled or used by the cast during production. The first group, often called *trim props,* would include items to give a room a "lived-in" look, such as ash trays, magazines, vases, books, fireplace irons, cushions, and so on. The second category, *hand props,* would include cigarettes, pistols, suitcases, coffee cups, banners, and the like. Arguments frequently occur among non-unionized crew members as to whether or not a piece of furniture is scenery or a property, or whether a sword is a part of a costume or a property. No final answer exists, and each producing agency must work out its own operating procedure. Rehearsals and performances can proceed smoothly only if a definite delegation of authority and responsibility exists under a central production concept.

A property crew, under the immediate direction of a property master, gathers, builds, sets, maintains, and strikes all items in this category. Property supervision demands imagination, organization, and creativity. Scripts may de-

146

mand almost anything. Memorable examples of property requirements include a mummy case, a Geiger counter capable of varying speed on cue, an aquarium full of live snakes, a live monkey on a leash, and an operable Hindu fakir's rope trick. No theatre could hope to have all possibilities covered in its storage rooms, so property acquisition often involves borrowing, renting, purchasing, or constructing various items. Property-rental agencies often have difficult items, but even their enormous resources can fail, in which case the producing company must either rewrite the script or substitute or construct a prop. Few companies do a more impressive job of property construction than the Tyrone Guthrie Company in Minneapolis or the Royal Shakespeare Company in London and Stratford-upon-Avon.

Careful selection of properties adds an important dimension to any show, and in some cases, it can tip the scale between success and failure. Every actor and director has experienced some disaster because of inept procedures, usually carelessness. The author once attended a production of *You Can't Take It with You* starring Imogene Coca. Ms. Coca was on stage alone as the show opened. The property crew had secured two kittens on leashes to a desk top, as suggested by the script, but as the stage lights came up one of the kittens fell off the front of the desk and was hanging by its leash, slowly strangling, as Ms. Coca began the scene. Because the production was on a thrust stage, a horrified audience member reached out and placed the kitten back on the desk. Until the kittens were removed, though, no audience member could look at anything else on the stage. The next night the crew substituted shorter leashes, and the show opened more smoothly.

Although some such stories are amusing in retrospect, they rarely entertain at the time, having eroded the concentrated work of many people. In extreme cases, the careless handling of firearms has resulted in the death of cast and crew members.

147

STAGE MAKEUP

Stage makeup has two purposes: to alter the facial characteristics of the actor (often including the hands, the neck, and other portions of the body) and/or to intensify the actor's features to overcome the high intensity lights, which may wash out his physical features. To achieve these purposes, a great number of materials, ranging from grease paint to plastics, are used. Their successful use has become a subart within the theatre, requiring constant practice and substantial skill.

Every actor should learn to make himself up for a straight role, but complex makeup designs may require the services of a specialist. In any event, the audience should not notice the makeup on the actor under stage lights, unless the character would normally wear excessive cosmetics, as some clowns or prostitutes might. In highly theatrical productions, such as *Stop the World, I Want to Get Off,* the production may make special demands with regard to makeup.

Successful makeup design and execution demands as much skill as portraiture because a complex makeup design is just that, a portrait overlaid upon the actor's face. Attempts to simplify the task do not often succeed. The young actor in an older role who resorts to black lines across the forehead to represent wrinkles and shoe polish to gray the hair does not give the impression of age; he gives the impression of having black lines across his forehead and shoe polish in his hair. Few scripts call for this effect.

Motion pictures, with their demands for verisimilitude in close-up photography, have stimulated new and better makeup techniques. Many of these techniques have been assimilated by theatre artists, who continue to study and experiment in this unique field. Like the other elements of design, stage makeup can add much to a production; it can likewise dilute the effect of an otherwise excellent play.

148

SOUND EFFECTS

Few audience members give much thought to theatrical sound effects. Even fewer would consider them a part of stage design. But for most shows, sound effects, which include music as well as the audible representation of devices or events, must be conceived, selected, and designed as a part of the total production. Directors and sound technicians confer to decide what will be used, as well as how much of the sound effects will be created live and how much recorded. Live effects usually work better for such items as offstage doors, single gun shots, falling bodies, door bells, telephones, and the like. Recorded sound often works better for such effects as explosions, trains, cars, parades, crowds, rocket launchings, and thunder. Music may be either live or recorded, depending upon the production budget, the demands of the script, and the director's preference.

With the recent advent of high fidelity, stereophonic, and four-channel sound for home-entertainment systems, higher-quality and more flexible equipment has become widely available. Nonprofessional technicians sometimes amass considerable knowledge about sound equipment. Sound equipment is expensive and demands considerable training for successful operation and maintenance. The author once saw an actor playing the title role in MacLeish's *J.B.* writhing in torment center stage and crying out, "Show me my sin, oh, God!" The script calls for God to answer, but God's voice had been taped so that a special electronic effect could be achieved. When the tape deck failed because of faulty maintenance, the actor's faith in God, the theatre, and electronics shriveled visibly. Happily a quick-witted technician snatched up a script and thundered a reply, substituting for Jehovah, and the scene survived. It did not, however, prosper. Sound technicians share the same terrors as other theatre artists. The missed cue, the equipment failure, the inept technician, can all completely destroy the work created by upwards of a hundred people laboring for months. One oversight can obliterate a production beyond redemption.

Conclusions

All phases of the technical theatre require expertise, craft, imagination, artistry, and responsibility. Whereas some actors and directors have thought (and some still think) that technical theatre has as its only function to enhance the confrontation between actor and audience, in recent years the technical theatre's contribution has emerged as comparable to that of acting, directing, and playwriting. The future seems to promise a more balanced view of the theatre, and theatre artists of all sorts as well as audiences can only benefit from the more comprehensive vision of the theatre.

Chapter Six

☆

The Theatre Architect

"But pardon, gentles all,
The flat unraised spirits that have dared
On this unworthy scaffold to bring forth
So great an object: can this cockpit hold
The vasty fields of France? or may we cram
Within this wooden O the very casques
That did affright the air at Agincourt?"
—*Henry V,* Prologue, lines 8–14

THEATRE artists do not require a theatre in order to create theatre, as evidenced by the production history of the past as well as by contemporary staging practices. Primitive societies perform dance dramas in any available open space, and throughout theatre history, companies have performed wherever they could, from the great halls of medieval castles to converted tennis courts. Perhaps the great Spanish playwright Lope de Vega put it best when he called for merely "four trestles, four boards, two actors, and a passion."

In modern times, producers have staged performances in a wide variety of places, including the main lobby of the Port Authority Bus Terminal in New York City, in streets, in museums, in living rooms, in theatre lobbies, in dormitory halls, and similar spaces. Especially after the advent of the "happening," theatre groups began to explore "found

151

space" for their performances rather than restricting themselves to theatres alone.

Nevertheless buildings designed specifically for performances house the vast majority of theatre events. Because the nature of the building affects how audiences will receive the play and determines many staging options, an examination of architectural considerations can contribute to a fuller understanding of how theatre happens.

Interaction with Other Theatrical Elements

The audience's specific reaction to the theatrical event begins as they approach the site of that event, that is, as they arrive at the theatre. Other considerations aside, the theatre's location and surroundings affect and concern the theatregoer. Ease in finding the theatre and in parking can obviously have considerable impact upon the audience member's attitudes and hence his reception of the production. The Loretto-Hilton Repertory Theatre in St. Louis, for example, has exceptionally fine architectural qualities and adequate parking facilities adjacent. The theatre is located, however, in Webster Groves, a suburb approximately ten miles from central St. Louis, and theatre patrons attending the Loretto-Hilton for the first time frequently encounter considerable difficulty finding the theatre. The Loretto-Hilton's substantial success attests to its artistic merit, but the company had first to educate its public as to its location. By contrast, the Tyrone Guthrie Theatre is easily accessible to central Minneapolis, as is the American Conservatory Theatre to San Franciscans.

Many other seemingly mundane matters affect a theatre facility's worth. Box-office location and the ease with which one can obtain tickets seems obvious, but in many theatres one must stand in long lines if the show has popular appeal.

152

Support facilities for the audience, such as coat checks, rest rooms, public telephones, drinking fountains, refreshment stands, and clearly marked aisles, all contribute either positively or negatively. (One might note that the personnel involved in the front-of-the-house operation are equally important; a surly or inept usher or concessionaire can alienate many patrons in a short time.)ᐟ

The size and design of the lobby area affects an audience's state of mind before a show and during intermissions. Most lobbies cannot contain a capacity audience, and some offer only bleak, sterile spaces in which to mill about. Producing agencies can do little about a theatre's basic architecture, but some decorate the lobby space with materials concerning their production or their season, whetting their patrons' theatrical appetites to return. Others present graphic art displays for the appreciation of those passing through. Both techniques indicate concern and respect for theatre patrons.

Another set of considerations emerges as an audience moves into the auditorium. Aisles that audiences can use easily and safely expedite crowd flow and control. Comfortable seats are important, and architects should remember to allow for wheelchair seating. The room between the rows of seats determines how many seats will fit into a given space and therefore affects audience capacity. Such matters frequently stimulate heated discussions between architects and business managers during design conferences.

Before the production begins, the audience should find the auditorium decor pleasing but not distracting. When the performance begins, concentration should focus on the playing area. Similarly, when the play begins, the architectural design should isolate the audience from external events, especially with regard to sound. Neighboring music practice rooms, outside traffic, lobby conversations, nearby rehearsals, or audible cues from stage manager to technicians distract an audience. Acoustical isolation requires material and space. These problems invariably return to

153

haunt the producer. The reader may have experienced inferior motion-picture-theatre architecture in which the viewer watches one movie while hearing two.

Theatre artists usually concern themselves primarily with the playing space or the stage and the support areas because they do most of their work there. Obviously the size of the stage itself affects the nature of the shows done there; small stages constrict large shows, such as *Hello, Dolly!* or *Mame.* Perhaps not so obvious to audience members is the need for space adjacent to the stage, the wings to either side and the flies directly above the stage. In multiset productions, the scenery may seem to appear and disappear by magic, but in fact technicians move it on from storage space and return it to the same space. The theatre architect must design such space into the building to facilitate the safe and efficient movement of such scenic elements. Figures 6-1a, 6-1b, and 6-1c illustrate three floor plans with three very distinct sets of production potentials. The author had directed and designed on all three stages.

Locations for hanging lighting equipment modify the lighting designer's options, as previously noted. Hardware upon which to hang the units and electrical outlets of sufficient number and power capacity must be built into the building to facilitate matters. Considering only one aspect of this problem, front lighting (the lighting that comes from the ceiling of the auditorium in the traditional theatre), compare Figures 5-6a and 5-6b in Chapter Five. In the Southern Illinois University theatre, as one stands on the stage and looks into the auditorium, one sees that a lighting instrument can be placed almost anywhere. At the University of Missouri, architects included only one beam slot or ceiling slot, so that technicians have had to rig additional pipes from the house lighting units to obtain the variety and number of lighting positions desired.

The placement of the lighting control board constitutes another major concern. In many older theatres, the control board is backstage; this location requires less cable to con-

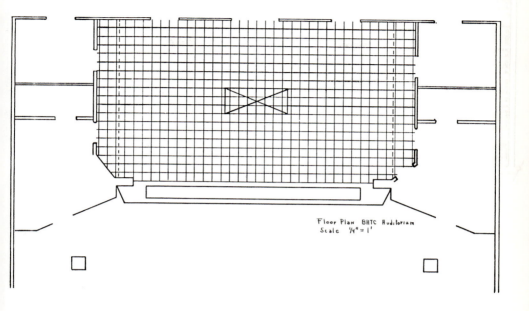

FIGURE 6-1A. *A floor plan of a stage at Black Hills State College. The squares inscribed on the stage floor each represent 1 square foot; the proscenium arch is 27½ feet wide and the stage is 19 feet deep, with relatively little wing space. The designer is thus faced with somewhat limited resources. The rectangle with diagonal lines represents a stage trap. From the author's personal collection.*

nect, hence less expense. But from such a site, the board operator can rarely see the stage and has no way of seeing the results of his work, detecting errors, or taking sight cues such as an actor's switching on a wall switch. In more modern theatres (see Figure 6-2), the lighting technician has a clear and unimpeded view of the stage and communicates with the stage manager by intercom, simplifying the entire situation considerably.

Other support areas of major concern include the scenery shop, the costume shop, semipermanent storage space,

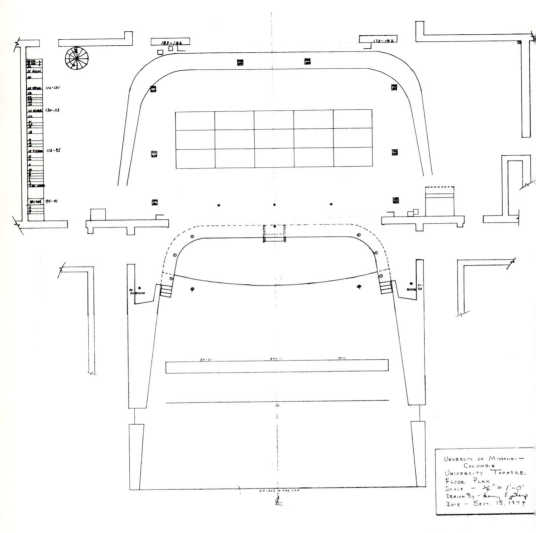

FIGURE 6-1B. *A floor plan of the stage at the University of Missouri—Columbia. In contrast to the stage at Black Hills State, this stage's proscenium arch is 38 feet wide, the depth of the stage is 43 feet, and ample wing space is provided on either side. The rectangles in the center represent stage traps; the two curved lines represent cycloramas. From the author's personal collection.*

FIGURE 6-1C. *Floor plan and side elevation of the University Theatre at Southern Illinois University—Edwardsville. This theatre (see also Figure 5-6A) is unusual in that it contains box seats and caliper side stages. From the author's personal collection.*

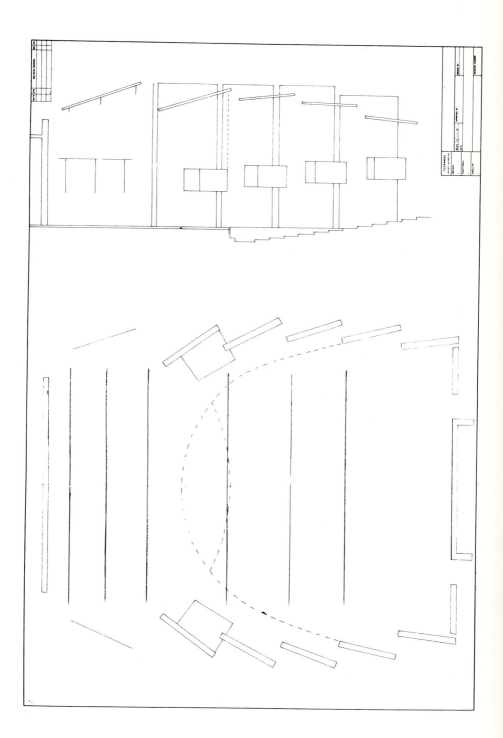

FIGURE 6-2. *The lighting technician's view of the stage, looking across the board. This is the same board shown in Figure 5-6C. Photograph by the author.*

makeup rooms, and dressing rooms. The doors between the scenery shop and the stage will limit the size of scenic elements. Although big doors cost more than little doors, stage hands frequently need to move large scenic elements from the shop to the stage.

Costumes usually come in more manageable sizes, but costumers prefer to have their shops convenient to the stage. They also prefer to have construction areas of adequate size. Most costume shops hamper and confine the costumer's efforts. Architects should also provide space for scenery storage, as well as storage for costumes, properties, lighting instruments, furniture, and makeup. Dressing rooms ought to allow convenient access to the stage. Ideally they have intercoms to the stage manager so that that person can relay information to the entire cast rapidly.

In educational theatre, the architect must also consider additional rehearsal spaces, classrooms, and offices. Staff and faculty sizes and preferences change. The effective architect seeks flexibility in his building, and many architects succeed admirably.

Figures 6-3a, 6-3b, and 6-3c illustrate some variations of configurations. The City Center Theatre in New York City, remodeled from the Mecca Temple in 1944, seats nearly 2,800; the farthest seats are 114 feet from the stage. The

FIGURE 6-3A. *The City Center, New York City. An enormous metropolitan theatre, best suited to dance, opera, and similar spectacles. Permission from the Theatre Collection, The New York Public Library at Lincoln Center; Astor, Lenox and Tilden Foundations.*

Tyrone Guthrie Theatre in Minneapolis, built in 1963, seats 1,437, but because of the thrust configuration and the wraparound seating arrangement, the farthest seat is only 52 feet from the playing area. Both these theatres house professional productions. The University of Iowa's theatre, built in 1936, seats only 500, and the farthest seat is 56 feet from the stage. Only 172 seats are available in one of the earliest permanent arena stages, the Penthouse Theatre at the University of Washington, built in 1940, and no one is farther than three rows from the playing area. All concerned with the planning of a theatre must clearly articulate and agree upon the intentions for the space in order to reconcile commercial and artistic considerations. If the space must serve multiple purposes, housing opera, lecturers, dance concerts, rock groups, and films, as well as theatrical

FIGURE 6-3B. *The Tyrone Guthrie Theatre, Minneapolis, Minnesota. One of the more successful regional theatres, the Guthrie is highly regarded as an example of excellent modern theatre architecture. Permission from the Tyrone Guthrie Theatre.*

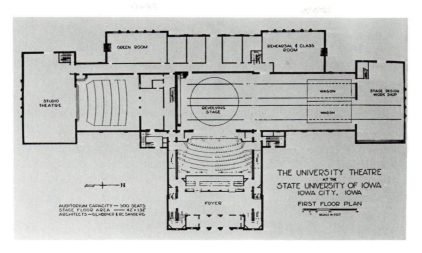

FIGURE 6-3C. *The University Theatre at the State University of Iowa. As described in the text, this theatre, although changed somewhat in actual construction, won wide approval. Note, however, that all wagons must come onto the stage from stage left, somewhat limiting shifting. Permission from the State University of Iowa.*

productions, the issues become even more complex. If, as in many high schools, the space must house basketball games and a cafeteria as well, rarely is anyone satisfied with the results.

The Architect's Alternatives and Restrictions

As we enter a theatre as audience members, we rarely concern ourselves with the architectural matters just described. The manifestations of architectural concerns influence us nevertheless. Thus the restrictions under which an architect must work may be examined for a fuller appreciation of his contributions.

161

Money looms up as the architect's first restriction. The amount of money with which he has to work is one of the most influential of factors and is usually the one furthest from his control, as the financing often comes from an outside source, such as a state government, a private group of investors, a grant, or a donation. The relativity of costs is illustrated by the theatres in Figures 6-3a, 6-3b, 6-3c, 6-3d, and 6-3e. Even considering economic fluctuations, building a theatre is costly: the Tyrone Guthrie Theatre cost $2.5 million, the University of Iowa theatre cost $240,000, and the Penthouse Theatre cost $64,328. More recent theatres may have cost much more. The University of Illinois in 1969 built the Krannert Center for the Performing Arts

FIGURE 6-3D. *The Penthouse Theatre at the University of Washington. This floor plan illustrates the intimacy of this theatre, no audience member being more than three rows from the acting area. Permission from the University of Washington.*

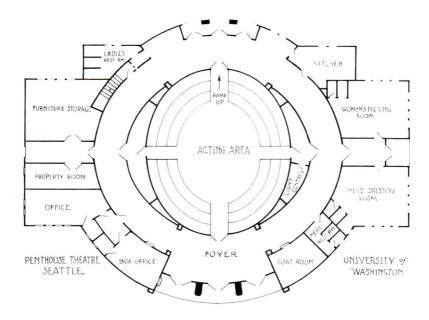

162

(Figure 6-4) at a cost of approximately $28 million, and the complex requires about $1 million a year for maintenance. The vast amounts of money required for modern construction of any sort demand careful and meticulous foresight and planning.

The size and nature of the construction site may affect the architect's choices. Building a new theatre in Times Square may involve real-estate prices of literally thousands of dollars per foot of frontage; prices elsewhere rarely reach such astronomical heights. Architects must consider the topography and the surroundings of a site as well when planning a design.

A building's financial backers usually indicate to an architect what configuration they wish in playing space and audience, a matter of immense impact upon theatre patrons. These configurations vary widely but are usually described as proscenium, thrust, arena, or flexible staging, each having distinct advantages and disadvantages.

FIGURE 6-3E. *The Penthouse Theatre at the University of Washington. This photograph was taken from the back, or third, row of the theatre and indicates the proximity of audience to playing area. Permission from the University of Washington.*

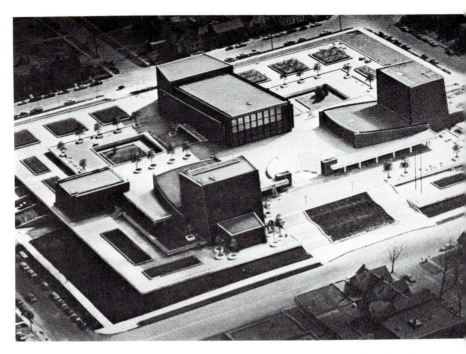

FIGURE 6-4. *The Krannert Center for the Performing Arts at the University of Illinois. This $28-million complex features five theatres: (1) the Great Hall in the upper center of the photo, used for concerts and motion pictures; (2) the Studio Theatre at the left, an experimental theatre (see Figure 6-7C); (3) the Festival Theatre at the right, which houses musical comedy and opera; (4) the Playhouse at the lower left, used for legitimate drama; and (5) the Amphitheatre at the lower center, which resembles classical Greek theatre architecture (see Figure 6-6) and also serves as steps leading to the upper mall. Permission from the Krannert Center for Performing Arts.*

PROSCENIUM STAGING

Since the Renaissance, the proscenium stage has been the most common form of theatre architecture. This "picture-frame" staging originated in the Italian Renaissance— specifically with the Teatro Farnese in Parma, built in 1618—when Italian architects, graphic artists, and theatrical

FIGURE 6-5A. *The Teatro Farnese in Parma, Italy. This theatre, which dates from 1618, contains what most scholars agree is the first permanent proscenium arch in the history of the theatre. Photograph by the author.*

designers became fascinated with perspective. The advantages of the proscenium configuration are thus primarily scenic; behind the curtain in a well-equipped theatre, the technicians can shift enormous amounts of scenery on and off the stage, dazzling the audience with spectacular effects. The disadvantages lie in the relatively small proportion of the audience near the stage and the resultant dilution of the actor's impact. Further, the presence of the architectural frame can inhibit interaction between performer and audience. Perhaps the proscenium configuration most resembles film; the presentation occurs in a rectangular frame.

THRUST STAGING

Modern theatre artists often prefer the thrust or three-quarter stage, exemplified by the Tyrone Guthrie and the

165

Loretto-Hilton theatres. With the upstage wall still offering considerable scenic potential, large audiences can watch from relative proximity by a seating arrangement extending to 180° or more around the sides of the acting platform. One might note that the two greatest periods of dramatic production of all time, those of fifth-century Athens and Elizabethan England, used the same arrangement, although audience capacities varied considerably. (See Figure 6-6.) Thrust staging leads to some problems of blocking; audiences in this configuration may find themselves looking at an actor's back more often than in proscenium staging, but directors have found numerous ways to counteract this difficulty.

FIGURE 6-5B. *The Loretto-Hilton Theatre at Webster College, St. Louis. An unusually flexible architectural design, the Loretto-Hilton offers both thrust and proscenium configurations. An orchestra can be placed in front of the stage for musical comedy or opera. Photograph by the author.*

FIGURE 6-6. *The Hellenistic theatre at Epidaurus, across the Saronic Gulf from Athens. This theatre is considered the best preserved of the classic theatres and is still used regularly for production (the stage setting seen here was for Aristophanes' The Clouds). Acoustics and sight lines allow all spectators an unimpeded reception of the production. Photograph by the author.*

ARENA STAGING

The arena configuration, or theatre-in-the-round, as exemplified by the Penthouse Theatre (Figures 6-3d and 6-3e), obviously puts more people closer to the playing area than any other arrangement, being the deployment a crowd will take around an event on an open, flat space. Primitive tribes usually surround the dance-drama area; modern sporting arenas typically employ this arrangement. Disadvantages emerge, however, when one considers that an actor's back will almost always be presented to some quadrant of the audience. Designers can offer only the most minimal scenic support to the action in most cases. For these reasons, arena staging has seemed more appropriate to experimental dramas not basically dependent upon de-lineation of locale. One cannot ignore the lower production costs for this staging method nor the relative ease of converting any open space into an arena theatre. Groups lacking a permanent theatre can employ arena staging to advantage in many cases.

FLEXIBLE STAGING

Flexible staging allows the director and the designer to choose proscenium, thrust, or arena configurations, following the unique demands of the script and their specific visions of it. Strictly speaking, flexible staging represents no particular form of audience–performer arrangement but rather an architectural scheme in which the playing space and the audience space are reconsidered for each production. Such theatres often employ banks of seats that are shifted into different patterns for different productions. Because of the logistics and the cost of such flexibility, theatres designed for flexible staging often have severely limited seating capacity.

One of the outstanding examples of such a concept of theatre architecture is found at the California Institute of the Arts, illustrated in Figures 6-7a and 6-7b. In essence, the Modular Theatre is a space 56 feet by 80 feet and 20 feet tall. The floor of the theatre consists of 4-foot-square panels capable of being raised by an air compressor up to 10 feet in elevation. Each of the modules can contain two swivel chairs. In effect, any part of the floor space can serve as playing area or audience area. Similarly the walls consist of 4-foot-square panels capable of hinging or removal in combination, adding still greater flexibility. Unhappily, financial difficulties have in effect stopped the theatre wing of the Institute, so the Modular Theatre, built for about $660,000, is seldom used today, nor was its potential explored while it was in use.

168

FIGURE 6-7A. *The Modular Theatre at the California Institute of the Arts in Valencia. As described in the text, this theatre is perhaps as totally flexible as a theatre can be. Each module can be raised or lowered, allowing the designer to determine the audience–acting area configuration anew for each production. Permission from the California Institute of the Arts.*

FIGURE 6-7B. *Another view of the Modular Theatre at the California Institute of the Arts, showing construction details. The power cords supply electricity for the aisle lights. Permission from the California Institute of the Arts.*

The Krannert Center for Performing Arts at the University of Illinois contains a comparable if less technologically astonishing flexible theatre. Called merely the Studio Theatre (Figure 6-7c), it is a large black room with movable seat banks and an overhead lighting grid.

Playwrights frequently write for a specific staging configuration. Although almost any script can conceivably be staged successfully in any of the above arrangements, the producing agency should select the configuration most appropriate for their production. To do this, the producers must have either a complex of several theatres or a single theatre capable of flexible staging. Both options have limitations: the multitheatre complex involves immense expense, and flexible staging can usually accommodate only small audiences. Professional producers often seek out an appropri-

FIGURE 6-7C. *The Studio Theatre of the Krannert Center for the Performing Arts at the University of Illinois. Although shown here in a proscenium type of configuration, this theatre can be reshaped for each production by deployment of seating banks. A lighting gridwork over the entire theatre offers comparable flexibility in stage lighting. Permission from the Krannert Center for the Performing Arts.*

ate theatre in which to present an intended production; educational producers often find themselves adapting a script to fit existing facilities. In either case, the impact of architecture has a massive effect upon theatrical production. The theatre artists responsible for placing a particular production in a specific space bear the responsibility for a successful marriage of the two. Those who attempt *Man of La Mancha* on a 10-foot-square platform in a dinner theatre run a considerable risk of achieving only a reductive and ineffectual version of the script's potential.

Requisites for Excellence in Theatre Architecture

Architecture is rightfully and traditionally classified as a fine art entirely separate from theatre. The theatre architect operates primarily as an architect and only secondarily as a theatre artist. His foremost concerns lie in his own art, not the art that will be created within his creation. Nevertheless, because form follows function, the excellence of his creation lies in large part in the functionality of the created form, or how well the theatre building facilitates the creation of theatre within it. Similarly one evaluates a school building, a home, an office complex, or a shop by its enhancement or hindrance of the events contained in it.

The theatre architect ought to bring to his work a simultaneously pragmatic and aesthetic imagination. The need for pragmatism stems from the scientific aspects of his art, which must follow the laws of physics, such as those concerning stress forces, erosion factors, weight allowances, surface durability, and tensile strengths. Less overtly scientific but equally practical concerns include construction economics, traffic patterns, color harmonies, texture preferences, and the availability of materials. Considering all these matters, the architect seeks to create a building of beauty, a

171

piece of "frozen music," as some have defined architecture. Viewers and users of the building should find it harmonious with its surrounding and within itself as well as utilitarian. Architectural aesthetics properly deserve treatment elsewhere, as it concerns the fine art of architecture rather than the fine art of theatre, but a work of architectural beauty offers a visual invitation to enter, a quality valuable to a theatre operation.

Another aspect of the architect's practicality centers on the inevitable need for compromise. Just as the theatre combines artistic input from numerous sources, and just as the conditions under which a theatre artist works determine much of what he can do, so too do conditions and people outside his immediate control modify much of the architect's work. Although, for example, he may have designed a theatre remarkable for its flexibility and beauty, if it cannot be paid for out of existing funds, his work comes to naught. If after he has made such a design, the people who will use the building have no use for it, again he has wasted his efforts. Tastes vary and finances dominate, so the architect's ideal may often be modified, diluted, and occasionally enhanced by others' input. His ability to deal with these circumstances may have as much effect upon the eventual outcome of his work as his aesthetic and practical abilities as a designer.

Obviously the architect needs considerable training. State laws require considerable formal training and an intensive examination before an architect is allowed to work. Just as in the theatre, training can foster talent but cannot substitute for it. For the theatre architect, further experience in and understanding of the art of the theatre will enhance his work considerably. Few architects receive training in theatrical production or appreciation, although as artists they often bring considerable understanding of the creative process to their assignments. For various reasons, funding agencies often hire a theatrical consultant to assist in and clarify the communications between the funding agency,

172

the theatre artists, the architects, and the contractors. If successful, the theatre consultant can add immeasurably to the eventual worth of the building.

The Contemporary Situation and Creative Procedures of the Theatre Architect

Architects will point out that their art is indeed the oldest art; mankind's need for shelter predates all other considerations of aesthetics. Architecture offers other unique qualities among the fine arts, being the only art in which a state license is required. In effect, there are no amateur architects. To be sure, a person may design and construct his own home, but public buildings, such as theatres, require by law the seal of an architect.

The architect (from *archi*, Greek for "foremost, leading, or chief," and *tekton*, "worker") until recent years oversaw all aspects of the design and construction of buildings. Although in modern times increased technology and legal ramifications make such a procedure impossible, the architect must undergo rigorous training before his license examination. This training may begin with a liberal-arts bachelor's degree, followed by three or more years in a school of architecture, or it may begin with six or seven years of apprenticeship with a master architect. Typically almost a decade of study is required to prepare for the examinations, with six months of intensive review, much like the preparation for doctoral degrees, making up the final preparation.

The architect's licensing examinations commonly require four days and consist of seven sections: architectural design, site planning, structural design, building equipment, history and theory of architecture, professional administration, and building construction. Emphasis may shift slightly from

173

area to area of the country. Floridians may be more concerned with hurricanes, Californians with earthquakes, and Minnesotans with snow loads, but for the most part, the examinations are comparable across the nation.

The newly licensed architect usually affiliates with an architectural firm rather than striking out on his own. In the 1970 census, 55,000 architects were listed in the United States labor force, as were 10,000 architectural firms. Median earnings for architects for that year were about $13,500, whereas artists, writers, and entertainers averaged about $9,500. The chief architect on a project receives from 6 to 8 per cent of the total construction costs, but one must remember rather substantial overhead costs. Further, the architect cannot, according to his code of ethics, advertise; he builds his reputation within a firm until he can be given more substantial projects.

Creative procedures for the architect should begin with the clients at the very first stages of planning, long before contracts are signed or bids let. Customarily the client first feels the need for a building and pursues the required funding. The architect can suggest from the very first the type of construction that can be achieved under the circumstances and indeed whether or not the building in question is feasible. This stage of planning requires a marriage of minds, and most architects agree that the clients are their single most productive resource; architecture, when successful, often reflects the clients far more than the architect. As in the theatre, excellence requires communication, modification, and compromise.

Eventually, if all goes well, the architects and the clients agree on a general plan, and the architect faces blank paper and begins to plan a building. He has certain finite considerations (in a theatre, for example, the desired number of seats and the specific audience–actor configuration). With these in mind, he begins to rough out his proportions with the related functional relationships. Like setting designers, some architects prefer to work in two dimensions with floor

174

plans and perspective drawings, whereas some prefer to work in three dimensions with models. Critics have accused some architects of working (like actors) from the inside out, arranging the functional elements of a building and then encasing it, while others have been accused of the opposite, designing the exterior of a building, and then forcing the various elements into that shell. Obviously the excellent architect does all these things simultaneously, marrying form and function in an integrated and organic entity of aesthetic value.

The architect takes his first designs back to the clients. There follows a long series of conferences for approvals and compromises until hopefully all are satisfied. Then, and only then, does the architect begin the long task of drawing up the formal plans for the building, the blueprints from which the building will actually be constructed. Errors here will, of course, result in errors in the building, so the architect must proceed with extreme care.

From these blueprints, the bids from the contractors are let, again a most sensitive stage for the eventual building. Here the architect's expertise in drawing up his formal blueprints, his knowledge of building materials, and his relationship with the contractors can make the difference between excellence and disaster. The legal responsibilities are also extremely complex. The architect should be on the construction site much of the time so that all will proceed smoothly.

Eventually all concerned make a final inspection, and the building is turned over to the client. Especially in theatre construction, there follows a period of "shaking down" the building, that is, learning to use the building and finding the inevitable malfunctions and unpleasant surprises. Here all the planning and conferences pay off. If all concerned have proceeded wisely and well, the building should serve the client's needs admirably. But even if the planning has not been well done and no matter how bad the building may be, the contractors do not tear it down and start over.

175

Too much money is involved, and the clients must live with the results. Misunderstandings and misinterpretations among those concerned with theatre construction can and do lead to lawsuits in extreme cases. These are unfortunate enough in themselves, but the eventual loser is the audience. The opportunity to build a theatre is not a responsibility to be taken lightly.

Evaluating the Architect's Contribution

Most of the concerns affecting an audience or a producing agency—location, lobby, support facilities, and so on—have been covered earlier in this chapter. Two other matters, however, deal with misuse of the theatrical space and emerge from the theatre artists' choice of scripts for production.

Sometimes a play will be chosen that the theatre building overwhelms. Specifically a so-called "small" script may be attempted in too large a theatre. The script *Summertree* by Ronald Cowan has occasionally suffered from such treatment. The script concerns a young man who wishes to study music but instead, because of parental pressure, is drafted into the army and is killed in Vietnam. Critics have suggested that the script comes perilously close to soap opera and excessive sentimentality; a few productions of *Summertree* have achieved its potential. *Summertree* premiered at the Vivian Beaumont Theatre at Lincoln Center in New York, a magnificent theatre, but perhaps too large for such a script. Some productions, done in intimate staging configurations with an audience of one hundred or less, however, have provided moving and effective theatre. Scripts that depend upon subtle and low-key performances may not be staged in mammoth theatres without a considerable risk of failure.

176

A more common judgmental indiscretion emerges from the attempt to put a "large" script in a small space. In the recently emerging dinner theatres across the country, large rooms are frequently employed to house the diners with the production staged on platforms set up in the room, usually in a thrust or arena configuration, achieving an intimacy that modern audiences have found entertaining. Insofar as the script depends upon lavish staging, however, such an arrangement is fraught with danger, as the resultant production may not achieve its potential. *Cabaret* exemplifies such a script, as might *Hello Dolly!, Mame,* or *Gypsy*. Managements have produced financially successful shows of this nature under such circumstances, but a production designed specifically for lavish proscenium staging will offer severe problems to one attempting the same script in arena or thrust configurations. The solution to those problems depends upon the imagination, talent, and resources of the theatre artists, but those problems can be beyond the capacities of all concerned, frustrating everyone, including the audience.

Certainly the architect cannot accept blame for either of the circumstances just discussed; his work is done long before script selection. Ideally, however, the work of the architect and of the theatre artist are wedded as the producers consider the spatial facilities in which they must work.

Conclusions

Predictions of future developments in theatre construction usually suggest that architects will seek more flexibility in audience–performer configurations, that theatre artists will grow less concerned with traditional staging, and that more multitheatre complexes will be constructed. Rising costs may force more and more imaginative use of existing

177

structures and more use of nontheatrical spaces. In any event, a much greater degree of communication, awareness, and planning should dominate future theatre construction. The waste of money would be reason enough for this, but the comfort of audiences and the encouragement of artistic creativity would benefit all concerned in the future. No one can predict with certainty what directions the theatre may take during the next generation. The theatre architect, now more than ever, must stay attuned to theatrical developments as well as traditions if he is to house the living theatre with efficiency and harmony.

Chapter Seven

Criticism

"The critic's symbol should be the tumble-bug; he deposits his egg in somebody else's dung, otherwise he could not hatch it."

—MARK TWAIN, *Mark Twain's Notebook*

To those outside the theatre (and often to those in it), the relationship between theatre artists and critics seems utterly hostile. If a critic attacks a performer for "running the gamut of emotion from A to B," the actor may call the critic "a legless man who teaches running." If the critic suggests that a certain actor "played the King as though fearful that someone might play the Ace," the critic may be called "a virgin teaching Don Juan how to make love." If in a production of *Uncle Tom's Cabin* a critic suggests that the bloodhounds were poorly supported by the cast, someone will probably quote Alfred, Lord Tennyson in describing the critic as "A louse in the locks of literature." Hardly any performer escapes negative criticism, and hardly any critic escapes the scathing scorn of theatre artists.

Yet critics continue to operate in the modern theatre, and they show no signs of dying out. The theatre has always had its critical observers, in one form or another, from Aristotle's work in classical Greece to the newspaper reviews of

179

FIGURE 7-1. *Critiques, reviews, and publicity releases, as illustrated in this montage, supply a record of the theatre's heritage as well as communication to potential patrons. Photograph by the author.*

next week's opening night on Broadway. Just as the spectrum of theatrical activity covers a multitude of possibilities, theatrical criticism also varies widely in form and function.

Modern theatre artists seek continually to evaluate themselves and their work. Only the most foolhardy find continual satisfaction in self-contemplation. But two external critical sources have great impact in today's theatre; the professional critics' reviews and the tangible response of the theatregoer. The professional critic offers an abstract reply to the production that in fact affects the theatregoer's ac-

180

tions, and the theatregoer's response is in the most concrete of terms, attendance in the theatre, usually affecting the financial circumstances of the producing agency. Under such circumstances, any examination of the theatre should include the critical conditions of the time.

The Professional Critic

Most theatregoers equate the professional critic with the reviews they find in newspapers and magazines or on television or radio. In larger metropolitan areas, these critics wield considerable power over the success or failure of commercial productions. In New York City, for example, their impact upon the Broadway and Off-Broadway theatre can hardly be exaggerated.

Before proceeding further, some semantic distinction between the terms "critique" and "review" may prove useful. Strictly speaking, no clear distinction exists in the dictionary sense, but theatre workers often consider the review a more journalistic endeavor, that is, the reporting and impression of a theatrical event. The critique, on the other hand, often implies a more penetrating analysis of the production in question. Theatre personnel, however, do not agree on these descriptions and regularly use the terms interchangeably.

TYPES OF CRITICS

The professional newspaper critic usually attends the opening night of a production and writes his review immediately thereafter for publication the next day. Broadway casts traditionally wait into the wee hours of the morning to read such reviews, which in large part determine their immediate future. If the reviews are especially bad, the show may not have a second performance. If they are quite good, the producers and publicists reproduce them and spread them around through all available media. More commonly, the reviews are mixed, partly positive and partly negative, in which case carefully selected portions appear in the publicity.

Critics whose reviews appear in magazines or in Sunday newspapers can take more time to prepare their work. Because such critics can work more carefully, these critiques often tend to be more thoughtful and polished. As well, editors usually allot more space for such items, allowing deeper analyses.

Media critics are a recent development. Some metropolitan broadcasting stations allot a few minutes of time for theatrical reviews on late-night news programs and repeat them the next day. The media reviewer often works under the same deadline pressure as the newspaper reviewer in order to get the material onto the air while it's still fresh. Little more than an impression can be given under these circumstances.

A fourth category of critics, not usually considered by the theatregoer, are the analysts, those critics who examine scripts in greater detail, often in book-length publications. Examples would include Martin Esslin's *The Theatre of the Absurd,* an important work in which the author examines an entire genre of scripts. Another example is Jan Kott's excellent *The Eating of the Gods: An Interpretation of Greek Tragedy,* a volume that took the author some six years to complete. Kott dealt with another style of drama in *Shakespeare, Our Contemporary.* Such analyst-critics may take up the work of a single playwright, a particular period of dramatic history, a genre of drama, or even drama in general.

THE FUNCTIONS OF CRITICISM

By now, the reader may have begun to deduce the functions of the critic and criticism from the types of critics and the forms they employ. At the most elementary level, a review should function as a news item, reporting that a specific company in a particular theatre staged a specified script. At this point, the reviewer usually includes for how long the play will be performed and where the theatregoer can obtain tickets. Media and newspaper reviews usually serve this function but often go beyond.

A second function of the critique is to present the reader with the critic's impression of the theatrical event. He may at this point describe the production style, the audience response, and the work's overall nature. The careful critic will not, however, confuse this function with the next.

An assessment of the production's value may appear in reviews. Here the critic must go beyond his impression of the work in isolation and consider it against his total theatregoing experience and his concepts of what the theatre at its best can be. At this point, the critic is most responsible and most vulnerable with his work; here he can make his greatest contribution to the theatre. The great critics of the past rose to eminence in this way. Lessing, for example, served as critic for a professional company in Germany in the eighteenth century. Although the productions are long since forgotten, modern theatre artists still find Lessing's essays of great value. Similarly Aristotle's analyses of the theatre of his day form a body of critical literature that no modern critic or theatre artist can ignore.

Two justifications for theatrical criticism seem obvious. First, critical response offers the only substantial reply to the theatre artist. Productions certainly succeed or fail at the box office in terms of audience attendance, but the perceptive and objective critic can help explain to the producing agency why they succeeded or failed. In a sense, the good critic can illuminate the public response for the producers and give them the only concrete reply for their work. Similarly gallery audiences may or may not attend showings of a painter's work, and the work may or may not sell, but the critic has the opportunity and responsibility to pursue the matter directly with the artist. Indeed it is his business to do so.

But critics do not write for the artists alone; most of the critic's audience is in fact the artist's audience. The critic can serve the higher purposes of theatre by illuminating the work for the actual or potential audience. Such a function does not demean the audience or suggest that they are too stupid to understand what they have seen. It rather implies that expert assistance may increase understanding and therefore appreciation. If the reader has ever sought or obtained an explanation for a difficult bit of writing, cinema, or painting, for example, he will appreciate this critical function. We may seek to grasp the nuances of modern art through trial and error, but understanding may come much sooner if someone helps clear the way.

The work of Henrik Ibsen, for example, stirred up great controversy in the later nineteenth century; many considered Ibsen a pornographer. Some critiques called his work "unnatural, immoral," "morbid and unwholesome," "an open drain; a loathsome sore unbandaged," "a bad escape of moral sewer-gas." The work of two English theatre critics, Bernard Shaw (later to become an outstanding playwright himself) and William Archer (who translated much of Ibsen's work into English), put the Ibsen canon in a new light and paved the way for future successes.

The Requirements of Criticism

Some critics win widespread respect, both among their colleagues and among theatre artists. Circumstances vary, but the qualities of the excellent critic commonly include the following.

1. *Love of the Theatre.* That a theatrical critic might not enjoy attending the theatre may seem incredible, but the record of the past suggests that such an unhappy state of affairs can indeed exist. A newspaper editor may, for ex-

184

ample, assign the theatrical beat to a reporter in addition to his various other duties, and that reporter may or may not be ready, willing, or able to review productions capably. Enthusiasm for one's work seems a requisite for excellence in any endeavor. If a theatrical critic has lost his sense of value for the theatre, he will have little to offer. If he never had it to begin with, he should seek other assignments.

2. *Fairness.* Any critic criticizes himself in that anyone expressing opinions or value judgments on any subject reveals his own prejudices and propensities. A critic cannot eliminate these human frailties, but he can attempt to minimize them as he prepares his reviews. If he sees on consecutive evenings a Greek tragedy, a musical comedy, a Shakespearean comedy, an Absurdist drama, a Neil Simon play, and a Chekhovian production, he might find difficulty in applying the same objective standards to them all. The excellent critics face this problem often and find personal means to solve it.

3. *Theatrical Experience.* A theatrical critic should have a considerable awareness of the heritage and the evolution of the theatre, as well as substantial insights into contemporary developments. The highly regarded Walter Kerr, Sunday drama critic for the *New York Times,* for example, began as a film critic for two newspapers while in high school. He later directed some fifty plays as a drama professor, and wrote or collaborated on several Broadway plays and musicals. Having served as drama critic for *Commonweal* for two years and for the New York *Herald-Tribune* for fifteen, he then joined the *Times*.

4. *Writing Skills.* The theatrical critic reaches his audience primarily through the written word. He should therefore have substantial ability to articulate his observations precisely. His writing circumstances may vary from the solitude of his study to the back seat of a speeding New York taxi as he tries to make a deadline, but his work will influence a number of theatregoers. Such responsibility demands accuracy and precision.

185

5. *Concentration*. Like the actor, the critic must ignore matters irrelevant to the production and concentrate upon the matter at hand. An audience member may let his mind wander or he may be troubled by something in his personal life, but the critic cannot allow himself this luxury because his response will be public. Outstanding critics must have the mental discipline necessary for intense, concentrated perception.

CRITICAL PREFERENCES

People's preferences vary widely in most matters; automobiles, music, clothing, hair styles, politics, sex, and religion, for example. It should come as no surprise to find that different people, either critics or ordinary citizens, have different expectations in the theatre. Audience members attend the theatre for different reasons, and they tend to evaluate the experience positively to the extent that the production meets their expectations. Specific artworks often have distinct dominant qualities, which tend to attract those audiences who most appreciate them. An individual audience member, then, may find the primary source of his appreciation of a production based on one or more of the following aspects.

1. *Appreciation of Pleasure*. Nothing is more difficult to define or less necessary to justify than pleasure. We are reminded of Goethe's statement on entertainment as a function of art. Whatever seems good to an audience member is, as far as he is concerned, good. But the very terms *good* represents only an indefinite commendation, a subjective response. If the production captures the agreeable attention of the viewer for a few hours, it has served a viable function for him. As we have seen earlier, a specific person may derive pleasure from more than mere diversion, but even diversion need not be mindless unless the audience is equally mindless, which is rarely the case.

186

2. *Appreciation of Impact.* Some audience members equate value in the theatre or in other art forms with the intensity of their emotional response. Such people often find themselves attracted to more serious drama, such as the classical tragedies, usually seeking a greater personal involvement in the artistic experience than is offered by milder forms of art. In other arts, such a person may find himself more attracted to Rodin's sculptures, Beethoven's symphonies, Wagner's music-drama, Goya's paintings, and similar works.

3. *Appreciation of Form.* Another type of artistic satisfaction, sometimes considered more sophisticated than the previous two, grows from the perception of the integration of artistic elements or the internal relatedness of the artwork. The appreciation of verse, for example, can stem from this aspect of artistry; the poet accepts the formal challenge of foot and meter and then creates within that framework. In the visual arts, the mobile offers a striking parallel; each piece literally counterbalances every other piece in a mutually dependent configuration of elements leading to an overall impression. Bach fugues appeal to many listeners because of their complex internal structure and the implication that the manner of execution may be as satisfying as the content.

Most of us find a propensity within ourselves to one or more of these aspects, and we tend to seek those qualities in our artistic experiences. Some artists have similar inclinations in their creativity. But the enduring artworks tend to amalgamate all three aspects and thus offer rich potential for all who experience them. Nor are the three aspects mutually exclusive; rather they offer three relatively identifiable responses.

The thoughtful theatregoer does well to examine his own preferences, lest he find himself totally "out of sync" with a production. This possibility represents a very real danger for the publishing critic; he may inadvertently divert an artwork from its intended audience or completely misinterpret it.

187

Suggestions for Theatregoers

Attending the theatre is as risky as watching sporting events; the viewer may from time to time find entertainment of the highest level, or he may be bored senseless. That is the chance one takes, but the theatregoer can increase the odds considerably by some fairly simple techniques.

1. First, find out something about the production before you go. Publicity releases try to entice you into the theatre, but they also describe to some extent the sort of event you may anticipate. Published reviews sometimes offer some insight, but critics can make mistakes. If you live in an area in which critics regularly cover theatrical productions, you might begin to see if their likes and dislikes correspond with yours and make your selections accordingly.

If the script is not a new one, you can usually find out its general nature fairly easily. If it is a new script, the producing agency will often be happy to describe it to you. But don't ask them what the play is about. Ask them what happens in it and what sort of script it is, and you'll usually get much more sensible answers.

Above all, the most effective means of theatrical publicity and the most effective means of learning about a production is "word of mouth." Nothing brings customers into a theatre like satisfied audience members, and nothing keeps them away like disgruntled theatregoers. Your friends, especially because they are your friends, can help you considerably in making your choices in the theatre.

2. Go to the theatre with an open mind and try to meet the production at least halfway. Much of what you see will no doubt be imperfect, and a certain school of critics and audience condemns everything. This sort of cynicism has no place in the theatre or any other art form, nor is it productive in any aspect of human endeavor. The other side of the coin is the attitude that everything is just wonderful; such a

188

view is equally counterproductive and unrealistic. But don't knock the show till you've tried it.

3. Most people prefer to go to the theatre with someone rather than alone. The theatre offers nothing if it doesn't offer sharing an experience; to share it with friends seems to enlarge artistic appreciation.

4. On behalf of theatre workers and audience members everywhere, let me take this opportunity to suggest that while you're in a theatre during a performance, keep quiet and listen. You will no doubt someday find yourself watching a production that you consider beneath contempt; the normal response is to tell someone. Or you may simply have succumbed to the habits of television and drive-in movie patrons, who too often keep up a line of chatter while viewing. In either case, I can assure you that a production is never so bad that someone doesn't enjoy it, just as it is rarely so good that someone doesn't hate it. Give the rest of the audience a chance; do not destroy the work's potential. If you don't like what is taking place on stage, leave. If you can hold out, wait till intermission to leave. If you hated the show, you can let the cast and producing agency know in more substantial ways. Theatrical productions are complex interactions, usually requiring intense concentration on the part of audience and performers alike. If you are unwilling or unable to enter into that contract with the performance, have the courtesy to let the cast and the rest of the audience try.

5. Consider giving the producing agency some feedback. Tell them or write them and let them know what you thought about their work. They may disagree, and they may not take your advice, but they will not ignore it. In selecting and preparing production schedules, producing agencies try to predict the future and read the minds of their audiences. This difficult task would be greatly facilitated if audiences would make their opinions known. Critics offer one sort of response, but the public can offer a very substantial one.

6. Don't be discouraged if you encounter a streak of dis-

agreeable theatre. Teams have losing streaks and individuals have slumps and bad semesters, but the effort usually continues. Producing agencies have bad years, but as long as they keep producing, the hope remains that things will get better. Hang in there.

Finally, theatre needs audiences for its survival, and in large part it tends to get the audiences it deserves. Perhaps not all audiences need theatre; the functions of art and the theatre exist in many and various human activities. But for twenty-five centuries, since Thespis stepped out of the Athenian chorus and began to enact Dionysus, the theatre has offered a uniquely direct form of aesthetic enjoyment to millions of human beings. As long as people seek vital interaction with other people, the theatre will continue to delight and stimulate its patrons. Perhaps some of you will never again enter a theatre, and you may live happy, prosperous, and productive lives without the theatre. But if you are still intrigued by the actions and interactions of humanity, the theatre has much to offer you.

Glossary

Actors Equity Association, 1500 Broadway, New York, New York 10036. Founded in 1912, this union serves as a bargaining agency for professional actors.

Actors Studio, 432 West 44 Street, New York, New York 10036. Founded in 1947 by Lee Strasberg (q.v.), Elia Kazan, and Cheryl Crawford, this actors' training institution bases much of its work on the Stanislavski System and the Method.

Aeschylus. (525–456 B.C.). Greek dramatist, said to have written ninety plays, only seven of which are extant, the best known being the Oresteian trilogy (*Agamemnon, Choëphoroe,* and *Eumenides*).

Aesthetics. That branch of philosophy dealing with beauty, emotion, and feeling as opposed to pure intellectualism.

American College Theatre Festival. An annual festival during which plays staged on college and university campuses may advance to state, regional, and national festivals, sponsored by the American Theatre Association (q.v.). Emphasis is placed on participation rather than competition, although awards are given in acting, playwriting, and scenic design.

American Theatre Association. A national organization open to anyone interested in theatre. The ATA contains within it seven divisions: the American Community Theatre Association, the Army Theatre Arts Association, the Children's Theatre Association of America, the National Association of Schools of Theatre, the University and College Theatre Association, and the University Resident Theatre Association. The central offices are located at 1029 Vermont Avenue N.W., Washington, D.C. 20005.

Anouihl, Jean (born 1910). Contemporary French dramatist, whose best-known works include *Antigone* and *The Waltz of the Toreadors.*

Appia, Adolphe (1862–1928). Swiss scenic and lighting designer whose innovations revolutionized stage production in Europe and America.

Aristophanes (ca. 448–380 B.C.). Greek dramatist and one of the outstanding comic playwrights of all time. His best-known work is perhaps *Lysistrata.*

Aristotle (384–322 B.C.). Greek philosopher and scientist whose *Poetics* analyzed tragedy and is studied widely today.

Atkinson, Brooks (born 1894). From 1925 to 1942 and from 1946 to 1960 the drama critic for the *New York Times.* Widely admired, Atkinson won a Pulitzer Prize for journalism in 1947 and is the only drama critic to have a theatre named after him. Author of *Broadway,* a history of the New York theatre.

Batten. In its most common usage, a pipe suspended from the flies (q.v.), to which scenery and lighting equipment may be attached to facilitate movement and shifting.

Bibienas. A family of Italian scene designers of the seventeenth and eighteenth centuries who introduced many innovations and reforms into scenic design at that time.

192

Blocking. A term usually referring to the overall traffic patterns of actors upon a stage; entrances, exits, movements, and so on. Cf. *Business*.

Brecht, Bertolt (1898–1956). A German playwright, usually associated with the Epic Theatre, whose best-known works are *Mother Courage* and *The Three-penny Opera*. A proponent of didactic drama (q.v.).

British National Theatre. See *National Theatre*.

Broadway, Broadway Theatre. Broadway itself is a street running diagonally across Manhattan in New York City, crossing Seventh Avenue at Times Square, the heart of the theatre district. *Broadway theatre* usually refers to the professional theatre in that area, although very few of the theatres are actually on Broadway itself. Cf. *Off-Broadway*.

Brook, Peter (born 1925). Outstanding British director whose most famous production was the world-acclaimed *A Midsummer Night's Dream*. Author of *The Empty Space,* a highly regarded treatise on theatrical theory.

Business. Besides the obvious financial meanings, in a general sense all stage movement and action. As more commonly used, the term refers to smaller actions, for example, lighting a cigarette, reading a book, or drawing a weapon.

Chekhov, Anton (1860–1904). Russian dramatist of outstanding merit, most of whose work was associated with Stanislavski and the Moscow Art Theatre (q.v.). His best-known works include *The Cherry Orchard* and *The Seagull*.

Chiaroscuro. A term from the graphic arts indicating the depiction of a subject in such a way as to give the impression of three dimensions, hence light and shadow.

Children's Theatre. Productions presented either by children or by adults for child audiences. Cf. *Creative Dramatics*.

Commedia dell'arte. A form of Italian folk theatre that flourished from the sixteenth to the eighteenth century. Unique in that most action and dialogue was improvised

193

rather than written and memorized. The character Harlequin still appears on the modern stage.

Community Theatre. Avocational theatre, that is, theatre performed not by commercial professionals nor by students but by community citizens. Permanent hired directors and staff are growing more common in the larger community theatres.

Craig, Edward Gordon (1872–1966). English scene designer and a prolific writer on matters theatrical. Associated with the "New Stagecraft" and with Appia (q.v.) Although considered impractical by some theatre artists, his controversial writings have caused many to consider him one of the leading theorists of this century.

Creative Dramatics. Although practitioners vary widely in their usage of this term, most consider it theatre by children that may or may not be presented to the public. Cf. *Children's Theatre.*

Cue. A signal for a technician or an actor. An actor's cue to enter the stage setting, for example, is often a line from another actor; the cue for a lighting technician to adjust stage lighting may be an actor's touching a light switch.

Cyclorama. A large, usually curved cloth or plaster device behind the scenery, used to represent the sky.

Didactic. Instructive, or intended to teach. Thus, in drama, scripts in which the purpose of edification is primary.

Diderot, Denis (1713–1784). French man of letters whose contributions to the theatre include several plays of the *drame larmoyant* (tearful drama) type and his *Le Paradoxe sur le comédien,* which addressed the degree to which an actor should feel actual emotion while performing.

Dimmer. An electronic device connected to stage lights, allowing technicians to vary the intensity of stage illumination.

Dionysus. A Greek god of nature, god of fertility and wine, roughly equivalent to the Roman deity Bacchus. It was during the celebrations to Dionysus that dramatic contests emerged in Greece, beginning in 534 B.C.

Dithyrambs. Choral hymns of praise to Dionysus (q.v.), thought by some scholars to be one of the main ingredients in the rise of drama in Greece.

Drame. Although rarely used today, this French term was used earlier to describe a play that was neither tragedy nor comedy but a mixture of the two, usually tending more toward the serious.

Educational Theatre. Theatre associated with institutions of learning, especially universities, colleges, junior colleges, and high schools.

Elizabethan Age. Literally, the period of reign of Elizabeth I of England (1558–1603), during which time Shakespeare, Jonson, and Marlowe led English dramatists to an unequaled literary excellence. Although the reign of James I (1603–1625) is called the Jacobean Age and the reign of Charles I (1625–1642) the Carolinian, some refer loosely to all three ages as the Elizabethan.

Equity. See *Actors Equity Association.*

Existentialism. Modern philosophy associated in drama with the Theatre of the Absurd (q.v.). Existentialism varies widely among its many proponents, chief among whom are Albert Camus (1913–1960), who stressed the absurdity of life, and Jean-Paul Sartre (born 1905), who maintained that existence precedes essence and that each person is responsible for his existence and all aspects of it, except for his responsibility.

Expressionism. A literary movement that developed before and after World War I in Germany, spreading thence to other nations. Expressionism seeks to portray inner emotions of human beings and thus is opposed to realism and naturalism (q.v.).

195

Farce. A comedic form seeking primarily to amuse. Comedy in the narrowest sense seeks a more thoughtful amusement, whereas farce seeks the release found in laughter.

Feydeau, Georges (1862–1921). French dramatist, a specialist in farces (q.v.), the best known of which is *A Flea in Her Ear*.

Fine Arts. Traditionally, architecture, literature, painting, sculpture, music, dance, and theatre. One should especially note the distinction between literature and theatre.

Fly, Flies. In theatre construction, the *flies* refers to that area above the stage itself into which scenery or lighting may be lifted. The act of elevating scenery into that area is called *flying*. Not all modern theatres have this facility.

Form. A term used frequently in two connotations, first as literary type or kind, as in the form of drama or the form of the novel. Drama as a general form may be said to contain the subforms of tragedy, comedy, farce, and so on. The term is also used to describe the arrangement of structure of materials within an artwork, thus the ordering principle. Cf. *Style*.

Found Space. A term used to describe space in which theatrical events are staged but that was designed for another purpose. Productions in the streets, bus terminals, gymnasiums, parks, and the like are said to use found space.

French Scenes. A term referring to the habit of the French dramatists in times past to mark the entrance or exit of a character with a scene division. Still used by some directors in script analysis.

Fresnel. A widely used stage-lighting instrument, named after the inventor of the stepped lens common to such instruments. Casts a pool of light with soft edges (cf. *Leko*) facilitating blending with the light of other instruments.

Gel, Gelatin. Many of the color filters placed over stage-lighting instruments are made of rolled gelatin, hence the use of these terms for any such filter, although plastic filters are becoming more common.

Gillette, William (1885–1937). American actor and dramatist whose greatest successes were in *Sherlock Holmes* and his Civil War spy dramas, *Held by the Enemy* and *Secret Service*.

Globe Theatre. The Elizabethan public theatre with which Shakespeare is most commonly associated. Built on the south bank of the Thames River in London in 1599, the theatre burned and was replaced in 1613 and was eventually pulled down in 1644.

Goethe, Johann Wolfgang von (1749–1832). Germany's greatest literary figure and a major playwright of all time, especially noted for *Faust*. A man of many talents and interests, Goethe also addressed himself lucidly to problems of aesthetics and dramatic theory.

Guthrie, Sir Tyrone (1900–1971). After a long and distinguished career in England, the United States, and Canada, in 1963 this noted British director opened the theatre in Minneapolis that bears his name.

Happening. An unstructured, frequently improvised avant-garde event with some theatrical overtones that emerged during the late 1950s. At the time, wide interest raised significant questions about the nature of art.

HB Studio, 120 Bank Street, New York, New York 10014. One of the more highly regarded actors' training schools, founded by Berghof in 1946, who was joined by his wife, the highly successful Uta Hagen, the following year.

Ibsen, Henrik (1828–1905). Norwegian dramatist who won international fame as one of the leaders of the realistic movement in drama, although he did not restrict himself to that type of drama. His best-known plays are *Ghosts*, *Hedda Gabler,* and *A Doll's House.*

Irving, Sir Henry (1828–1906). The outstanding English actor–manager at the turn of this century, highly regarded

197

in many Shakespearean roles. Irving was the first English actor to receive knighthood.

Jones, Inigo (1573–1652). Considered by most the first English scene designer of note. Also an architect. Introduced proscenium (q.v.) staging to England.

Jonson, Ben (1572–1637). English playwright, contemporary of Shakespeare. Especially highly regarded as a comic playwright, his best-known script is *Volpone.*

Kean, Edmund (ca. 1787–1833). Outstanding English actor whose debut in London in 1814 marked the beginning of Romantic acting on the British stage. His acting reflected his fiery, tempestuous life.

Leko. A widely used theatrical lighting instrument using a planoconvex lens and a parabolic reflector. This instrument casts a sharply defined pool of light and is most useful in lighting the stage from some considerable distance.

Lessing, Gotthold Ephraim (1729–1781). German playwright and dramatic critic who sought with some success to free German literature from the Neoclassic regulations under which it suffered at the time. His best-known treatise is *The Hamburg Dramaturgy.*

Little Theatre Movement, The. A nation-wide movement, primarily in U.S. community theatres between 1910 and 1930, which attempted to utilize the European ideals of strong directing, non-commercial goals, and new staging techniques. See *The New Stagecraft.*

Long Run. Cf. *Repertory* and *Stock.* This phrase refers to the common practice in New York and elsewhere of running a production as long as money is made at the box office.

Loutherbourg, Philippe Jacques de (1740–1812). A French painter and scene designer who in 1771 joined forces with David Garrick, then the leading actor–manager in London, and proceeded to introduce numerous reforms and innovations in lighting and design.

Melodrama. Originally, drama with songs but now used to describe scripts seeking to excite audiences emotionally by sensation, suspense, spectacle, and frequently improbable events.

Moliére (1622–1673). Stage name of Jean Baptiste Poquelin, a French actor–manager–dramatist usually regarded as one of the comic geniuses of all time. *Tartuffe* and *The Miser* are among his better-known scripts.

Moscow Art Theatre. A famous Russian theatre, still in operation, founded in 1898 by Stanislavski (q.v.) and V. I. Nemirovich-Danchenko and the site of the major premieres of most of the plays of Anton Chekov (q.v.). Stanislavski's major contributions to the theatre were made during his tenure here.

National Theatre. Founded in 1963 with Laurence Olivier as its director, this is a government-subsidized theatre of Great Britain. Having won worldwide acclaim from the beginning, the company has recently opened a magnificent complex of theatres on the south bank of the Thames.

Naturalism. A literary and artistic approach that emerged in the latter half of the nineteenth century, growing out of the increasing scientism of the time. Although sharing realism's (q.v.) concern with external forms, naturalistic approaches tend to be even less selective.

Neoclassicism. A literary and artistic philosophy that emerged during the Renaissance (q.v.) and spread throughout western Europe, stimulated by the rebirth of interest in Greek and Roman cultures and the lessening of ecclesiastical domination of thought. Basically humanistic, Neoclassicism found man's greatest hope for earthly happiness in analysis and systematic thought.

New Stagecraft, The. An American term used to describe the non-traditional staging techniques first advanced in Europe by Craig (q.v.) and Appia (q.v.). Many of these innovations were first seen in this country as a part of the *Little Theatre Movement* (q.v.).

Nietzsche, Friedrich Wilhelm (1844–1900). German philosopher who wrote valuable and insightful treatises on the nature of art and tragedy.

Off-Broadway. Commercial theatre productions away from the central theatre district in New York (see *Broadway*) with somewhat lower production budgets. *Off-Off-Broadway* is an emerging term, referring to even less expensive and more experimental productions in New York. Distinctions are not sharply defined.

Olivier, Lord Laurence (born 1907). English actor, director, and producer, knighted in 1947 and in 1970 created a baron, the first actor to receive this honor. Among his many theatrical accomplishments, none rank higher than his successful direction of the National Theatre during its early years.

O'Neill, Eugene (1888–1953). Often considered the United States' best playwright. His best-known works include *The Emperor Jones, Desire Under the Elms,* and the autobiographical *Long Day's Journey into Night.*

Passion Plays. Ecclesiastical dramas dealing with the passion, death, and resurrection of Christ.

Phenomenology. A philosophical doctrine growing in modern acceptance, originated by Edmund Husserl (1859–1938). Not to be confused with its appearance in scientific usage, phenomenology is the science of all phenomena, the real things or the purely conceptual.

Plautus (254–184 B.C.). Roman dramatist whose style was marked by a coarse wit, rapid action, and a considerable insight into human affairs. His best-known works include the *Menaechmi* (the source of Shakespeare's *Comedy of Errors*) and *The Braggart Warrior.* Plautus influenced many later playwrights.

200

Plot. The organizing structure of the action in a drama. Organization by story is the most familiar but by no means the only type of plot. For a detailed discussion, see Smiley, *Playwriting: The Structure of Action,* especially Chapter Three.

Polyclitus the Younger. Although very little is known about his life, most scholars agree that he designed the theatre at Epidaurus, built during the second half of the fourth century B.C. This is the best preserved of the Greek theatres and is still used regularly for productions.

Presentational. Cf. *Representational.* A term sometimes used to describe theatrical productions that do not attempt to give the illusion of realism or naturalism (q.v.).

Producer. In the commercial theatre, that person or persons in overall charge of financial matters, usually the person or persons funding the production. The term is usually used to distinguish his role from that of the director, who has charge of all aesthetic decisions but who is hired by the producer.

Prompt Script. Usually the director's script, containing his notes, the blocking and cues for the show, and any other relevant material. This copy is used to prompt actors during rehearsals, hence the name.

Properties. Objects on the stage other than scenery, such as trim props (including curtains, pictures, and so on) and set props (including furniture, phones, and so on). Also includes items carried by the actors, or hand props.

Proscenium, Proscenium Arch. In theatres so constructed, the architectural arch that divides the audience area from the stage.

Protagonist. In Greek drama, the leading actor, now usually the "hero," or that character for whom the audience has most sympathy.

Realism. A theatrical movement that developed in the latter half of the nineteenth century that sought to depict nature and life with great fidelity. Scientism and positivism contributed considerably to the movement. Cf. *Naturalism.*

Regional Theatre. Permanent professional theatres outside New York City, such as San Francisco's American Conservatory Theatre, St. Louis's Loretto-Hilton, or Minneapolis's Guthrie Theatre.

Reinhardt, Max (1873–1943). Austrian manager and actor and an outstanding director whose most famous productions include *Oedipus Rex, Jedermann, The Miracle,* and *A Midsummer Night's Dream.*

Renaissance. That period of time, roughly from the fourteenth to the seventeenth century, marked by increases in humanism, learning, and classicism. Marks the break between the medieval and modern periods.

Repertory. Literally a collection of productions, more commonly a production scheme in which several plays are alternated by a company, as opposed to the long run or stock plan of production (q.v.).

Representational. Cf. *Presentational.* A style of production that seeks to create the illusion of reality of action and actual environments on stage. Usually associated with realism (q.v.).

Restoration, Restoration Drama. Literally the restoration of the English monarchy with Charles II in 1660. In literary history, the following period till about 1700. The drama of this period was a remarkable mixture of verbal wit and inverted moral values.

Romanticism. As a literary or theatrical movement, Romanticism emerged around 1800, extolling the virtues of natural instinct and the beauties of nature.

Royal Shakespeare Company. Like the National Theatre (q.v.), a government-subsidized British theatre company. The RSC, which tends to be somewhat more experimental than the National Theatre, operates theatres in London and Stratford-upon-Avon.

Runthrough. An uninterrupted rehearsal of a scene, an act, or an entire production, as opposed to those rehearsals in which directors or technicians stop the action to make adjustments.

Sabbattini, Nicola (ca. 1574–1654). Italian architect and scenic designer, also the author of *Pratica di fabricar scene e machine ne' teatri,* an important early treatise on production techniques.

Saxe-Meiningen, Duke of (1826–1914). German director whose company toured widely and influentially between 1874 and 1890. Although others had sought to insist upon the unified interaction of settings and performers, the duke is widely considered the first director in the modern sense.

Serlio, Sebastiano (1475–1554). Italian scene designer and architect whose revolutionary book *Regole generali di architettura* introduced perspective to the art of scenic design in 1545.

Shaw, George Bernard (1856–1950). English playwright, critic, and author. Shaw wrote brilliant, didactic dramas of wide popularity, the best known of which included *Pygmalion* (on which *My Fair Lady* was based), *Arms and the Man, Major Barbara,* and *Androcles and the Lion.*

Sheridan, Richard Brinsley (1751–1816). British dramatist and manager whose best-known plays are *The School for Scandal* and *The Rivals.*

Siddons, Mrs. Sarah (1755–1831). English actress, widely considered to have been the greatest tragic actress of the English stage. Her most successful role was Lady Macbeth. Her brother, John Philip Kemble, was also a leading performer of the time.

Soliloquy. A speech by a character on stage alone, usually designed to reveal his inner thoughts. The best-known example is Hamlet's "To be or not to be" soliloquy.

Sophocles (496–406 B.C.). Greek dramatist who presumably wrote over a hundred plays of which only seven are extant, including *Oedipus Rex* and *Antigone*.

Stanfield, Clarkson (1793–1867). English scene designer whose principal innovation was the diorama, a display of scenery.

Stanislavski, Konstantin Sergeivich (1865–1938). Russian actor, director, teacher, and author. Co-founder of the Moscow Art Theatre (q.v.) and originator of the Stanislavski System, an approach to acting that stresses the internal and psychological.

Stock. A production scheme in which several plays are presented for limited runs, as in summer stock, in which plays are given for a week or two and then replaced, as opposed to repertory or the long run (q.v.).

Stoppard, Tom (born 1937). Contemporary British playwright whose major successes include *Rozencrantz and Guildenstern Are Dead, Jumpers,* and *The Real Inspector Hound.*

Strasberg, Lee (born 1901). American actor, director, and teacher. One of the founders of the influential Group Theatre, later of the Actors Studio (q.v.), and a major, albeit controversial, influence upon American acting.

Style. An aggregate of characteristics common to a person, period, nationality, or dramatic type.

Subtext. A term associated with Stanislavski and Strasberg's philosophies of acting, referring to the line of internal thought that the actor discovers in analyzing and delivering his lines and actions.

Theatre of the Absurd. A term originated by Martin Esslin in a book by the same name, referring to dramas based on Existentialism (q.v.), such as those by Sartre, Ionesco, Camus, Genet, Adamov, Becket, Pinter, and so on.

Thespis. A Greek poet and actor of the sixth century B.C., traditionally considered the first actor and the founder of drama. He won first prize at the first drama festival held in Athens, ca. 534 B.C.

Torelli, Giacomo (1608–1678). The first professional scene designer who was not also a traditional painter. His scenic effects and innovations were widely admired, although some feared that he was in league with Satan.

Tragedy. A serious form of drama, the form of which varies widely in different periods but that usually ends with the protagonist (q.v.) destroyed socially or physically, although frequently winning a spiritual victory in defeat.

Type Casting. The casting of roles in a play by matching the most obvious characteristics of the actors to the characters.

United Scenic Artists. The Union for professional and scenic designers, lighting designers, and costume designers. Like Actors Equity Association (q.v.), the negotiating agent for its members. Founded in 1918.

United States Institute of Theatre Technology, 1501 Broadway, New York, New York 10036. A recent organization of those concerned with the technical theatre. Publisher of *Theatre Design and Technology,* circulated four times yearly.

Vaudeville. An immensely popular form of entertainment from about 1865 to the 1930s, consisting of a series of various acts, such as singers, dancers, comedians, acrobats, trained animals, dramatic sketches, and so on. The advent of motion pictures and radio killed this valuable training ground for performers, although the television variety show offers comparable appeals.

Vega, Lope de (1562–1635). Spanish playwright and the most prolific of all dramatists, credited with over 2,000 plays. Of the more than 400 extant scripts, the best known are *The Sheep Well* and *The Mayor of Zalamea.*

205

Vitruvius (fl. 70–15 B.C.). Roman historian of architecture whose *De Architectura* was of immense influence upon Renaissance theatre construction.

Voltaire (1694–1778). Pseudonym of François Marie Arouet, a Frenchman of letters and philosopher whose several plays and staging reforms had important effects upon the French stage.

Wilder, Thornton (1897–1976). American playwright and author whose plays include *The Skin of Our Teeth* (for which he won the Pulitzer Prize in 1943), *The Matchmaker,* and *Our Town.*

Wings. In a proscenium theatre, those areas on either side of the stage in which scenery may be stored. So called because of earlier drop and wing staging, the drop hanging at the back of the stage, the wings at the sides.

Bibliography

For Further Study
Aesthetics and Creativity

1. Fowles, John. *The Aristos.* New York: The New American Library, Inc., 1970. Written by a contemporary novelist (*The Magus, Daniel Martin, The Collector,* and *The French Lieutenant's Woman*), this volume presents an entire world vision, including the roles of science and art in modern society, in an innovative format that has found considerable favor among university students in all fields.

2. Koestler, Arthur. *The Act of Creation.* New York: Dell Publishing Co., Inc., 1964. A substantial and thorough treatment of creativity manifested in the total spectrum of human endeavor as perceived by one of the outstanding thinkers of our time.

3. Pirsig, Robert M. *Zen and the Art of Motorcycle Mainte-*

nance. New York: Bantam Books, Inc., 1974. A most remarkable and popular book. The subtitle, "An Inquiry into Values," indicates its relevance to aesthetics in modern society.

4. Stolnitz, Jerome. *Aesthetics*. New York: Macmillan Publishing Co., Inc., 1965. Professor Stolnitz has collected in this slim volume a series of particularly illuminating essays on art and aesthetics, not the least of which is his own introduction.

Theatrical Theory

1. Dukore, Bernard F. *Dramatic Theory and Criticism: Greeks to Growtowski*. New York: Holt, Rinehart & Winston, Inc., 1974. A massive source book of writings from the past and present on dramatic theory and criticism, with lucid introductions by Professor Dukore.

2. Schechner, Richard. *Public Domain*. New York: Avon Books, 1969. A series of essays and articles in which the author seeks to justify and explain modern theatre. Especially recommended is perhaps his best-known article, "Six Axioms for Environmental Theatre," in which he correlates public events and traditional theatre.

3. Selden, Samuel. *Man in His Theatre*. Chapel Hill: The University of North Carolina Press, 1957. Selden writes especially clearly about the origins of the theatre and its relevance to society by placing theatre in context with human action.

4. Shank, Theodore. *The Art of Dramatic Art*. Belmont, Calif.: The Dickenson Publishing Co., Inc., 1969. A most provocative book in which the author sets out to define the parameters of the theatre. A work that will inevitably stimulate considerable fruitful discussion.

5. Wright, Edward A., and Lenthiel H. Downs. *A Primer for Playgoers,* 2nd ed. Englewood Cliffs, N.J.: Prentice-Hall, Inc., 1969. An especially clear and insightful treatment of how the theatre happens.

Theatre History

1. Brockett, Oscar G. *History of the Theatre,* Boston: Allyn and Bacon, Inc., 1977. 3rd ed. The most popular one-volume text in theatre history today, this volume is well-illustrated and comprehensive in its scope and treatment of theatrical heritage.

2. Hartnoll, Phyllis. *A Concise History of the Theatre.* London: Thames and Hudson, 1968. Less comprehensive than Brockett's book, this volume is perhaps more appropriate to the newcomer to theatre history. It contains 262 illustrations, 34 of them in color.

3. Hewitt, Barnard. *History of the Theatre from 1800 to the Present.* New York: Random House, 1970. Written by one of the outstanding theatre scholars of recent years, this small volume treats the modern theatre with style and clarity.

4. Macgowan, Kenneth, and William Melnitz. *The Living Stage: A History of the World Theatre.* Englewood Cliffs, N.J.: Prentice-Hall, Inc., 1955. For many years this book was the most popular theatre history text used in colleges and universities; it still offers the reader eminently readable prose and accurate scholarship.

Playwriting

1. Cole, Toby, Ed. *Playwrights on Playwriting: The Meaning and Making of Modern Drama from Ibsen to Ionesco.* New York:

Hill and Wang, 1961. Available in paperback, this book compiles essays and observations on playwriting by the major dramatists of the past century.

2. Hart, Moss. *Act One*. New York: Signet Books, 1959. An especially readable and insightful autobiography by a recent American playwright.

3. Smiley, Sam. *Playwrighting: The Structure of Action*. Englewood Cliffs, N.J.: Prentice-Hall, Inc., 1971. The most popular of the current texts on playwriting. Professor Smiley, himself a published and produced playwright, covers the process of creating drama completely, offering the novice playwright much excellent advice.

4. Wager, Walter, Ed. *The Playwrights Speak*. New York: Dell Publishing Co., Inc., 1967. Similar to *Playwrights on Playwriting* by consisting of interviews with most of the major playwrights working today. Available in paperback.

Script Anthologies

1. Block, Haskell M., and Robert G. Shedd, Eds. *Masters of Modern Drama*. New York: Random House, 1962. A collection of forty-five scripts, most of them full-length, covering dramaturgy from Ibsen to the present day. Illustrated.

2. Dukore, Bernard F., Ed. *17 Plays: Sophocles to Baraka*. New York: Thomas Y. Crowell Co., 1976. This collection is much enhanced by Professor Dukore's astute introductions and annotated bibliographies. The volume is in paperback.

3. Gassner, John. *A Treasury of the Theatre,* various editions. New York: Simon and Schuster. Gassner (joined for the fourth edition by Dukore) compiled a two-volume set that has for years been the basis for college script-reading courses. The introductions and bibliographies again add much to the worth of the collection. Easily found in most libraries.

History of Dramatic Literature

1. Gassner, John. *Masters of the Drama,* 3rd ed. New York: Dover Publications, Inc., 1951. An immense (890 pp.) compilation, often used as a reference work or a text in theatre-history classes.

2. Nicoll, Allardyce. *World Drama from Aeschylus to Anouilh.* New York: Harcourt, Brace & World, Inc., n.d. Comparable to *Masters of the Drama,* this volume was written by one of the outstanding British scholars of theatre and drama.

Directing

1. Clurman, Harold. *On Directing.* New York: Macmillan Publishing Co., Inc., 1974. While not a "how-to" book, this paperback volume presents a sensible description of the director's work by a highly regarded professional director and theatre critic. Especially valuable are the sections of prompt scripts from plays directed by Clurman.

2. Cole, Toby, and Helen Krich Chinoy, Eds. *Directors on Directing: A Source Book of the Modern Theatre.* New York: The Bobbs-Merrill Co., Inc., 1963. Available in paperback, this volume contains a series of essays about and by the most famous directors of the past century. The first essay, "The Emergency of the Director," by Professor Chinoy, is an outstanding piece of scholarship and writing. An excellent bibliography is included.

3. Dean, Alexander, and Lawrence Carra. *Fundamentals of Play Directing,* 3rd ed. New York: Holt, Rinehart & Winston, Inc., 1974. An amplified edition of Dean's original work in 1941, long considered a standard text for beginning directing classes. Nicely illustrated, with a usable glossary of terms.

4. Hodge, Francis. *Play Directing: Analysis, Communication, and Style.* Englewood Cliffs, N.J.: Prentice-Hall, Inc., 1971. Perhaps the most widely used college directing text at the present time. Professor Hodge of the University of Texas is held in extremely high regard by colleagues and students alike.

5. Logan, Joshua. *Josh: My Up and Down, In and Out Life.* New York: Delacorte Press, 1976. In his autobiography, Logan describes in a most readable style how he rose to the top ranks of Broadway and Hollywood directing. A fascinating glimpse backstage.

Acting Theory

1. Chekhov, Michael. *To the Actor on the Technique of Acting.* New York: Harper and Row, 1953. Written by the son of Anton Chekhov, the great Russian playwright, this volume, although somewhat advanced for the beginning student, delineates clearly some of the more mystical and psychological aspects of acting.

2. Cole, Toby, and Helen Krich Chinoy. *Actors on Acting: The Theories, Techniques, and Practices of the Great Actors of All Times as Told in Their Own Words,* 3rd ed. New York: Crown Publishers, 1970. A key work in any study of acting theory and practice, this volume selects from the pivotal works on the subject from Plato in ancient Athens to Joseph Chaikin of the Open Theatre, which has only recently disbanded. The meticulous scholarship by the co-editors concludes with an outstanding bibliography.

3. Goldman, Michael. *The Actor's Freedom: Toward a Theory of Drama.* New York: The Viking Press, 1975. One of the more exciting recent publications on this subject, in which the author examines the actor in performance with perception and lucidity.

4. Hagen, Uta, with Haskel Frankel. *Respect for Acting.* New York: Macmillan Publishing Co., Inc., 1973. A book widely admired by actors at all levels of development, definitely pro-Method, written by an outstanding actress and teacher. Highly recommended.

5. Harris, Julie, with Barry Tarshis. *Julie Harris Talks to Young Actors.* New York: Lothrop, Lee, & Shepard Company, 1971. Miss Harris has achieved the highest pinnacles of theatrical success; in this volume she recalls her early frustrations and passes on to the would-be performer the enormous benefits of her experience. This volume is not to be overlooked by anyone considering a theatrical career.

6. Lewis, Robert. *Method—or Madness?* New York: Samuel French Inc., 1958. As the title implies, Mr. Lewis, one of New York's more successful directors, addresses himself to the controversies surrounding the Stanislavski System or Method. He does this with unusual clarity and awareness, giving advantages and disadvantages along the way.

7. McGaw, Charles. *Acting Is Believing: A Basic Method for Beginners.* New York: Holt, Rinehart, & Winston, 1964. This text has for a long time won the approval of many acting teachers for its simple and fundamental treatment of complex materials.

8. Stanislavski, Konstantin, translated by Elizabeth Hapgood. *An Actor Prepares.* New York: Theatre Arts Books, 1936. The key volume in the Stanislavski canon, the student must read this book if he is to assume knowledge of the Stanislavski System, either pro or con.

Actor Biographies

1. Leach, Joseph. *Bright Particular Star: The Life and Times of Charlotte Cushman.* New Haven and London: Yale University Press, 1970. Miss Cushman was the first American actress to achieve an international reputation for excellence. Professor Leach did immense amounts of research in the preparation of this excellent volume.

2. Moody, Richard. *Edwin Forrest, First Star of the American Stage.* New York: Alfred A. Knopf, 1960. In chronicling Forrest's life, Professor Moody set a standard of scholarship and writing that has seldom been equaled.

3. Prideaux, Tom. *Love or Nothing: The Life and Times of Ellen Terry.* New York: Charles Scribner's Sons, 1975. Ellen Terry was England's most popular actress at the turn of this century. Tom Prideaux, for decades theatre editor and critic for *Life* magazine, has written an outstanding evocation not only of Miss Terry but of daily life in the theatre in England at that time.

4. Ruggles, Eleanor. *Prince of Players: Edwin Booth.* New York: W. W. Norton and Co., Inc., 1953. Edwin Booth, the brother of Lincoln's assassin, is considered by many to have been America's greatest actor. Miss Ruggles has captured the spirit of this tortured artist in one of the outstanding theatrical biographies of all time. Although the volume is out of print, it is easily found in libraries and used-book stores, as it was a very popular Book-of-the-Month Club selection.

5. Skinner, Cornelia Otis. *Madame Sarah.* Boston: Houghton Mifflin Company, 1966. Sarah Bernhardt, the subject of this book, was perhaps the most controversial and popular performer of all time. Miss Skinner, herself an actress of the first rank, performed a labor of love in preparing this volume.

Scenic Design

1. Burdick, Elizabeth R., Peggy C. Hansen, and Brenda Zanger, Eds. *Contemporary Stage Design U.S.A.* Middletown,

Conn.: Wesleyan University Press, distributed for the International Theatre Institute of the United States, Inc., 1974. A handsome paperback with introductory essays of value and many illustrations, some in color, of contemporary scenic and costume designs.

2. Burian, Jarka. *The Scenography of Josef Svoboda.* Middletown, Conn.: Wesleyan University Press, 1971. Profusely illustrated, albeit in black and white. Professor Burian has described the work of the world's leading scenic designer with careful scholarship and exceptional lucidity. Especially interested students should be aware of Professor Burian's article "A Scenographer's Work: Josef Svoboda's Designs, 1971–1975," in *Theatre Design and Technology,* Volume XII, Number 2 (Summer, 1976), which covers Svoboda's work through those years.

3. Mielziner, Jo. *Designing for the Theatre: A Memoir and a Portfolio.* New York: Bramhall House, 1965. Beyond the implications of the title, Mielziner describes in considerable detail how he designed *Death of a Salesman.* Many theatre artists consider Mielziner the outstanding American scenic designer.

4. Parker, W. Oren, and Harvey K. Smith. *Scene Design and Stage Lighting,* 3rd ed. New York: Holt, Rinehart & Winston, Inc., 1974. Heavily illustrated, this text is extremely popular in stagecraft courses at the college and university level, as it covers the process of scenic design, executing the design, and designing the lighting. Considerable technical information is included.

Stage Lighting

1. Bellman, Willard F. *Lighting the Stage: Art and Practice,* 2nd ed. New York: Chandler Publishing Company, 1974. Although this book tends somewhat more toward practice than art, it has been extremely well received in colleges and universities as a text for lighting courses. Highly regarded.

Costume Design

1. Russell, Douglas A. *Stage Costume Design: Theory, Technique, and Style*. New York: Appleton-Century-Crofts, 1973. A reasonably complete "how-to" volume for the stage costumer, containing a useful outline history of Western costume and a glossary of terms.

Stage Makeup

1. Buchman, Herman. *Stage Makeup*. New York: Watson-Guptill Publications, n.d. Although not as widely used as the Corson book of the same title, this is a lavishly illustrated volume on makeup techniques, both simple and complex.

2. Corson, Richard. *Stage Makeup*. 5th ed. Englewood Cliffs, N.J.: Prentice-Hall, Inc., 1975. As the number of editions indicates, this volume has won wide acceptance. Somewhat more detailed than the Buchman book. Includes very valuable color plates.

Theatre Architecture

1. Silverman, Maxwell. *Contemporary Theatre Architecture*. New York: The New York Public Library, 1965. Silverman has compiled photos and plans of some fifty outstanding designs, both realized and projected. Ned. A. Bowman, an outstanding scholar in this field, has added 1,741 bibliographical items from 1946 to 1964.

2. Southern, Richard. *The Seven Ages of the Theatre.* New York: Hill and Wang, 1961. A Dramabook paperback volume. Southern has written primarily a theatre-history text, but his concern with actor–audience relationships makes this a valuable publication for the student of theatre architecture.

3. Tidworth, Simon. *Theatres: An Architectural and Cultural History.* New York: Praeger Publishers, 1973. This volume offers exactly what the title implies and includes 188 plates and a brief bibliography.

4. Young, William C. *Documents of American Theatre History: Famous American Playhouses,* 2 vols. Chicago, Ill.: American Library Association, 1973. Young surveys the major American theatres, past and present, including New York playhouses, regional theatres, college and university theatres, and summer playhouses.

5. Burris-Meyer, Harold, and Edward C. Cole. *Theatres and Auditoriums.* New York: Reinhold Publishing Corporation, 1949. Although now somewhat dated, this volume, prepared by two outstanding scholars, was long considered essential to theatre planning, and it still deserves the attention of anyone considering theatre construction.

217

Index

Numbers in italics refer to illustrations

A

O

P

Q

R

S

Y

Z